Daisy Alice Kugel

The Stout Institute Bulletin

Recipes for Food Classes

Daisy Alice Kugel

The Stout Institute Bulletin
Recipes for Food Classes

ISBN/EAN: 9783337211776

Printed in Europe, USA, Canada, Australia, Japan

Cover: Foto ©Andreas Hilbeck / pixelio.de

More available books at **www.hansebooks.com**

The Stout Institute Bulletin

Special Number
Recipes for Food Classes

Published at
Menomonie, Wisconsin

INTRODUCTION

The following recipes are used in The Stout Institute in the first year cookery classes. No originality is claimed for them. They are, for the most part, foundation recipes or proportions which may be found in every reliable cook book. Stress is placed upon the knowledge of proportions and of materials, rather than of recipes, in order that the student may become more practical and adaptable both in the teaching and the practice of cookery. The directions given are more detailed and specific than those given in cook books, such being necessary for class room use.

In every case where recipe and directions, or experiments, have been taken directly from another source, credit has been given.

I wish to thank Miss Florence Scoular and Miss Kathryn Bele, teachers of cookery in The Stout Institute, for their assistance in revising this manual.

DAISY ALICE KUGEL,
Director, School of Household Arts.

February, 1923.

Regulations for Food Laboratories

1. Wear clean uniforms, and aprons with pockets, and provide hand towels, holders and hair-nets.
2. Wash hands before beginning work in the laboratory.
3. No jewelry is permitted to be worn on the hands.
4. All dishes belonging to the dining room must be paid for if broken.
5. Utensils and dishes are not to be taken from the laboratory.
6. Leave desk top and bread board clean and dry.
7. Leave wood work of desk clean, i. e., front of desk and drawers.
8. Stove should be left clean as knife and paper can make it. Be sure to leave it dry that it may not rust.
9. Extinguish gas of burners and ovens when through using.
10. See that supply drawers are clean, and everything in place.
11. Wipe sifter with dry towel. Wash only when necessary and then dry thoroughly.
12. Leave all tools clean, and especially the steels, bright and dry.
13. Scour steels and pans with cork and scourer.
14. Do not soak steel knives and forks, nor wet gearing of Dover egg beater.
15. Turn knife edges to the left.
16. Place measuring cups with handles to the right.
17. Use care in opening and closing drawers that tools may remain in place.
18. Place saucepans and double boilers with handles to the right.
19. Do not use double boiler as a saucepan.
20. After using brush, wash and leave, brush side down, in the place provided for the purpose.
21. Place scraps of soap in soap shakers at the sink, and wash soap dishes.
22. Waste jars should be emptied and washed.
23. Wash towels and dish cloths, and hang on rack to dry in orderly manner.
24. Put paper, tin cans, and broken articles in incinerator.
25. See that floor in front of desk is clean, and tools in place before leaving laboratory.
26. Anything spilled on the floor must be wiped up with floor cloth provided.
27. Utility trays must NEVER be used for baking or cooking.
28. Outer garments must not be brought into the laboratory.
29. School supplies and books should never be placed on laboratory tables. They do not belong in the laboratory.
30. Stools must be in place before students leave the room.
31. Supplies on supply tables are to be kept covered when not in use.

4

DIRECTIONS FOR DISHWASHING

1. Scrape all dishes well, leaving no scraps to collect in dish water.
2. Wipe all greasy dishes with soft paper.
3. Soak all dishes that have contained flour mixtures, eggs, or starchy material in cold water.
4. Rinse in cold water all dishes that have contained milk or cream.
5. Soak in hot water, dishes that have contained syrup or sugar mixtures.
6. Place all dishes of a kind together and pile up neatly.
7. Have a clean dry place clear for clean dishes.
8. Have ready two pans—one containing hot, soapy water for washing dishes; the other filled with hot, clear water for rinsing.
9. Wash dishes in the following order: glassware, silverware, china, (washing cleanest first), small cooking utensils and frying pans.
10. Outside of kettles and frying pans should be washed as clean as inside.
11. Use Dutch cleanser or similar scourer with cork to remove food that sticks or is burnt on.
12. Use brush to clean sieves, strainers, ricers, etc.
13. Scour steel knives.
14. Do not put knife handles or cogs of Dover egg beater in water.
15. Wash dish pan and rinsing pan and wipe dry.

CARE OF TOWELS

1. Wash dish towels and dish cloths with hot water and soap. Rinse thoroughly in clear water, shake out, and dry, hanging towels straight. Both towels and cloths should be hung in light place to dry, not under sink or behind stoves, and should be boiled once a week.

THE GAS RANGE

A range of ordinary size has:

1. Four top burners, for sauce pans, kettles, etc.
2. One or two sets of oven burners for heating the ovens.
3. A baking oven for bread, cake, and large roasts.
4. A broiling oven (below the burners) with rack and pan for steaks, chops, etc., for small roasts, for toast and dishes to be browned.
5. Gas-cocks, one or more to each top burner, two to the oven burners to regulate the supply of gas.
6. An oven lighter or "pilot light" at the side of the oven for lighting the oven burners.
7. A stove pipe connected with the chimney for carrying away gases produced by combustion.

The broiling oven is heated directly from the oven burners, the baking oven by currents of heated air passing around it as in a coal range. Some ranges have a small top burner, called a simmering burner; all ranges should have a movable sheet of iron under the top burners. The connecting pipe is sometimes fitted with a gas cock.

Air is admitted to the burner through holes in the supply pipes. This makes the gas burn with a blue and very hot flame.—From William & Fisher "Elements of the Theory and Practice of Cookery."

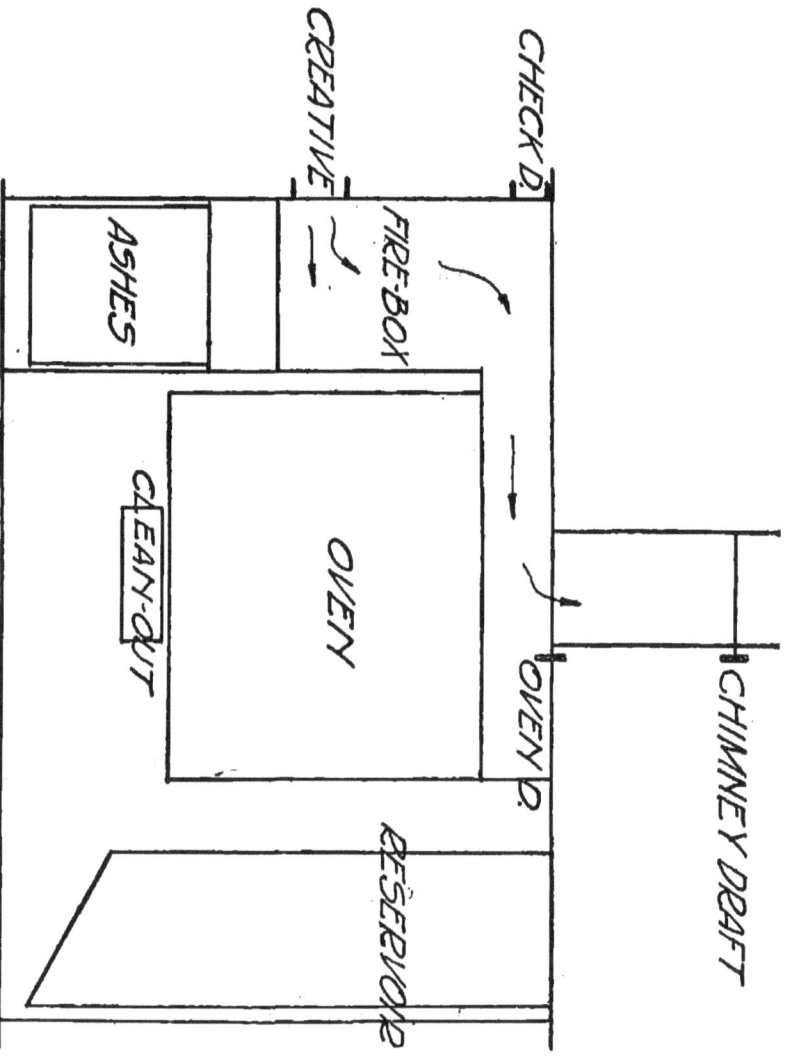

COAL AND WOOD RANGE
Parts of Range
1. Ash-pan.
2. Four dampers which are (a) creative draft; (b) check draft; (c) chimney damper; (d) oven damper; (e) reservoir damper.
3. Fire-box.
4. Grate, or floor of fire-box.
5. Ovens.
6. Stovepipe.
7. Top or cooking surface with lids.
8. Reservoir, though this is not always a part.
9. Clean-out.

To Start Fire
1. Arrange paper, kindling, and wood to permit circulation of air.
2. Open creative and chimney drafts.
3. Apply lighted match to papers.
4. Add more fuel when fire has good start.
5. Never fill fire-box more than two-thirds full.
6. Never use kerosene or gasoline to start fire.

To Regulate Fires
1. For a hot fire (a) open creative and chimney draft; (b) close oven damper; (c) keep fire-box two-thirds filled.
2. To heat oven (a) close oven damper, and chimney draft partially; (b) close check draft; (c) partially open creative draft.
3. To hold fire (a) fill fire-box; (b) close all dampers; (c) open check about halfway.
4. To heat reservoir, close reservoir damper.

BEVERAGES

1. .Prepare four cups of tea, A, B, C, D, in the following manner
   using black tea:
   A—1 level t tea, 1 c boiling water. Pour the boiling water
   through the tea leaves, but do not allow the tea leaves
   to remain in the cup.
   B—1 level t tea, 1 c boiling water. Pour the boiling water
   over the tea leaves and allow to stand over the leaves
   for 5 minutes. Decant off.
   C—Repeat B but do not decant the infusion. Allow it to
   cool and then reheat it.
   D—1 level t tea, 1 c boiling water. Pour the boiling water
   over the leaves and continue the boiling for 5 minutes.
   Note the color, odor and taste of each cup of tea.
2. Test 2 tb of each cup of tea with 5 drops of lead acetate.
   What change occurs? Due to what? What method brings the
least tannin into the infusion?

TEA

Scald an earthenware teapot, put tea in tea ball, allowing 1 t of
tea to each cup of freshly boiling water; pour over it the boiling
water, remove tea ball; cover closely; pour at once. Or, a silver or
nickel tea ball may be used in a cup. Allow the same proportion of
tea to water.

COFFEE EXPERIMENTS

1. Use coarsely ground coffee, 1 c cold water in coffee pot and
   bring to the boiling point and boil for 2 minutes. Let stand
   for 5 minutes.
2. Repeat 1 using coffee pot and bag.
3. Repeat 1 using percolator.
4. Repeat 1 using finely ground coffee.
5. Repeat 2 using finely ground coffee.
6. Repeat 3 using finely ground coffee.
7. Use coffee pot and bag, boiling for 5 minutes with coarse coffee.
8. Use coffee pot and bag, boiling for 5 minutes with fine coffee.
9. Use coffee pot, coarse coffee, and 1 tb egg white, 1 c cold water,
   and boil for 5 minutes.
10. Repeat 9 using finely ground coffee.
11. Repeat 1 using boiling water.
12. Repeat 2 using boiling water.
13. Repeat 3 using boiling water.
14. Repeat 4 using boiling water.
15. Repeat 5 using boiling water.
16. Repeat 6 using boiling water.
17. Test 2 tb of the coffee infusion made in each method with 5
   drops lead acetate. Is the presence of tannic acid shown?
   Compare methods, best method and modifications that may
   be made.

FILTERED COFFEE

½ c fine coffee   1 qt. boiling water
Put coffee into filter, and pour over it, gradually, the freshly
boiling water. After water filters through coffee (it must be kept

hot), pour off and return a second time, and sometimes a third time. Remove strainer before serving. If stronger coffee is desired, use ¼ c coffee for each cup water.

BOILED COFFEE

½ c coffee	½ c cold water
4 shells or 1 egg white	3½ c boiling water

The usual rule is 2 level or 1 rounded tablespoonful coffee and 1 egg shell for each cup of coffee served. Egg shells should be washed before eggs are broken. Mix broken shells, or egg white and 4 tb cold water (allow 1 tb for each cup) in well aired and scalded coffee pot. Add freshly boiling water and let boil five minutes after boiling begins. Pour 4 tb cold water down spout. Let stand five to ten minutes where it will keep hot, but not boil or simmer. Serve at once. It is usually best to strain from grounds into another coffee pot.

Many people consider that a speck of salt added to coffee improves the flavor.

Coffee is sometimes made with cold water instead of boiling water. In this case, mix coffee and egg, add requisite water and bring to boiling point. Remove from fire and "settle" with cold water. Let stand without boiling for about five minutes.

COCOA AND CHOCOLATE EXPERIMENTS

1. Prepare cocoa paste using 2 t cocoa and 2 tb hot water and 1 t sugar. Pour 1 c cold liquid on to the paste. Cook in the double boiler for 5 minutes.
2. Repeat using ¼ square of chocolate in place of the cocoa paste.
3. Repeat 1 using hot liquid and cooking for 5 minutes in double boiler.
4. Repeat 2 using hot liquid and cooking as in 3.
5. Repeat 3 and cook for 15 minutes.
6. Repeat 4 and cook for 15 minutes.
7. Prepare cocoa by cooking sugar, cocoa and half of the liquid directly over the fire until it begins to thicken. Then add remaining liquid and cook for 15 to 20 minutes in the double boiler.
8. Prepare as in 7 using chocolate in place of the cocoa.
9. Prepare as in 7 but add a grain of salt and two drops of vanilla.
10. Prepare as in 8 adding salt and vanilla as in 9.
11. Prepare as in 9 but beat with a Dover egg beater before serving.
12. Prepare as in 10 and use Dover egg beater as in 11.

Compare as to:
Flavor,
Sweetness,
Color,
Consistency,
Texture,
Method most desirable for the preparation of cocoa or chocolate.

COCOA

2 tb cocoa	1 pt. boiling water
2 tb sugar	1 pt. scalded milk
spk salt	

The general rule is ½ tb of cocoa and of sugar for each cup liquid (half each milk and water).

Mix sugar, cocoa and salt. Stir in boiling water, a very little at a time to mix well. Boil about five minutes, then combine with hot milk. Beat with egg beater before serving. Serve with additional sugar and cream, if desired. Cream may be whipped.

CHOCOLATE

2 oz. chocolate   1 pt. scalded milk
4 tb sugar   spk salt
1 pt. boiling water

Use ¼ square of chocolate and 1 tb sugar for each cup liquid. Break chocolate into pieces. Add sugar, salt and boiling water, and stir until smooth and glossy. Let cook about five minutes or until it begins to thicken. Add milk, and when well mixed cook over fire about five minutes, or cook slowly in double boiler for fifteen minutes.

Less water and more milk may be used, if desired. ½ t ground cinnamon may be mixed with either cocoa or chocolate when sugar is added, if additional flavor is liked. Or, ½ t vanilla may be added.

CEREALS

CEREAL EXPERIMENTS

1. Make the following tests with iodine:
   - ¼ t dry cornstarch
   - ¼ t moist cornstarch
   - ½ t cooked cornstarch.

   Observe the change in color. A blue, violet, or purple color indicates the presence of starch.

2. Make the same test with iodine, using the following cereals, cooked, moist and dry:

Rice	Cream of Wheat
Cornmeal	Wheat flour
Shredded wheat	Force

3. Wash a little rice and test the water with iodine. Result? Why do you observe a change?
   —Taken from "Laboratory Manual of Foods and Cookery," by Matteson & Newlands.

4. Cook a fourth of a cup of the following cereals in twice as much water and four times as much water as cereal. Results?

Oatmeal	Cream of Wheat
Rice	

5. Cook a fourth of a cup of cornmeal in four times as much water and in six times as much water as cereal. Result?

GENERAL DIRECTIONS

1. Pick over and wash whole cereals.
2. Pick over and soak coarse cereals.
3. Use 1 t salt to 1 qt. water for steamed cereals.
4. Use a double boiler.
5. Stir cereal, dropping it slowly into boiling, salted water.
6. Stir as little as possible while cooking.
7. Boil directly over heat for 3 to 5 minutes.
8. Finish over water.
9. When done, all the water should have been absorbed.
10. For variety, steam with the cereal well washed dates, figs, raisins, or dried apricots or peaches. Slices or sections of fresh apple, peaches, pears may be added during the last thirty or forty minutes of cooking. The steamed cereal may be served with any fruits previously stewed, or fresh fruits served over it. The cereal may be cooked in strained fruit juice or milk instead of water.
11. Left-over cereal may be moulded in a buttered bread pan, sliced when cold and sauted for luncheon or supper dish. It may also be molded in cups or individual molds and served with fruit and whipped cream or a pudding sauce for a simple dessert.

BOILED RICE

1 c rice   1 tb salt
2 qts. boiling water

Look over rice, wash in strainer or colander. Stir gradually into rapidly boiling water. Stir with fork at first to prevent sticking. Boil till tender or about twenty minutes, then drain thoroughly. If it is desired to have each grain separate, drain in strainer and pour over hot water to wash off starch. Return to kettle to heat and dry out or place in hot oven a few minutes. If left-overs are to be used for croquettes or molds this should not be done.

STEAMED RICE

1 c rice   ½ t salt
3 c boiling water or milk

To hot water or milk, or half of each in double boiler, add salt. Stir in rice previously looked over and washed. If water is used, cook directly over the flame a few minutes, place over water and cook till tender, about an hour.

SAUTEED CEREAL

Turn hot cereal into granite or aluminum pan, rinsed in cold water. Let stand until thoroughly chilled, and firm. Remove cereal from mold by inverting over plate and tapping on bottom. Cut into slices (a cord may be used) half inch thick. Dip in salted flour or in slightly beaten egg. Put into hot frying pan and saute until brown.

TABLE SHOWING PROPORTION OF WATER AND TIME FOR COOKING CEREAL

Oatmeal	4 c water to 1 c cereal	3 to 6 hours
Rolled Oats	3 to 4 c water to 1 c cereal	½ to 6 hours
Rice (boiled)	8 c water to 1 c cereal	25 to 30 min.
Rice (steamed)	3 or 4 c water to 1 c cereal	1 hour
Wheat (rolled)	1½ c water to 1 c cereal	1 hour
Wheat (granular)	3 to 4 c water to 1 c cereal	1 to 3 hours
Corn Meal	6 c water to 1 c cereal	3 to 6 hours
Cracked Wheat	6 c water to 1 c cereal	3 to 6 hours
Hominy	4 c water to 1 c cereal	2 to 4 hours

FRUITS

STEWED FRUIT—GENERAL DIRECTIONS

1. Use half as much water as fruit.
2. Use ¼ or ½ c sugar for 2 c fruit.
3. Cook sugar and water to form a syrup.
4. Add fruit, cook till tender.
5. Remove fruit and boil down syrup, adding spice or lemon if desired.
6. If fruit is hard like quinces or pears, cook first in water, not adding sugar until tender.

APPLE SAUCE

Pare, core and slice apples and cook in water until tender, then add sugar. From ¼ to 1/3 cup sugar may be added to each cup of sauce depending upon the tartness of the apples.

PEAR COMPOTE

6 pears	8 tb sugar
2 c boiling water	2 tb lemon juice

Pare and core fruit and place in cold water to prevent discoloration till ready to use. Make syrup, add fruit cored side down. Boil gently until soft but not broken, add lemon juice just before done. Cook small quantity at a time.

COOKED RHUBARB

Wash, peel and cut rhubarb in one inch pieces. If pink and tender do not peel, as the color is much better if the skin is left on. Add just enough water to keep from burning. When nearly done add sugar to taste. Cook until tender.

Or, the rhubarb may be put in kettle with an equal weight (half as much by measure) of sugar, and allowed to stand for several hours until sugar is nearly dissolved. No additional water will be necessary. Cook uncovered in double boiler.

Or, cut rhubarb into earthen or agate dish. Mix with sugar, 1/3 to ½ as much sugar as rhubarb. Add 1 to 2 tb water, cover closely and set in oven. Cook till rhubarb is tender.

A bit of white ginger root, or orange peel may be added to either stewed or baked rhubarb. Figs, dates, or raisins, previously boiled in hot water, may be added.

CRANBERRIES

1 qt. cranberries	1¾ c sugar
1 c water	

The general rule is: Use one-fourth as much water as cranberries. Add one-third as much sugar as cranberries.

Have water boiling. Add berries, cover, and cook slowly till berries have burst outer skin. Add sugar and boil few minutes longer. Pour into mould. If desired, cranberries may be steamed before sugar is added.

BAKED APPLES

6 apples   2/3 c boiling water
6 tb light brown sugar

Select smooth uniform sized apples. Wash and core. Fill the centers with sugar. Place in shallow pan, pour water about them, bake till tender, twenty to forty minutes according to size and variety of apples. Baste while baking. A little lemon juice or cinnamon may be added for flavor. Chopped nuts or raisins may be mixed with sugar for filling apples.

PRUNE PUFF OR SOUFFLE

1 c chopped or strained prunes   ¼ c powdered sugar
3 egg whites

Use cooked prunes. Chop up fine or put through strainer. Beat egg whites stiff, add powdered sugar slowly, beating all the time. Fold into prunes. Place in buttered pudding dish, set dish in pan of hot water, and bake in moderate oven about 20 minutes, or longer. Serve with soft custard made with yolks of eggs, or with whipped cream.

Other dried fruit may be used instead of prunes.

PRUNES

Wash, soak over night. Heat gradually in water in which they are soaked, and cook slowly (on back of range or over asbestos mat), closely covered, till skins are tender, letting water cook away till syrup is thick. They are best cooked in earthen jar, slowly for six hours. Most prunes contain so much sugar that lemon juice improves the flavor. Seldom do they need sugar.

BREADS

Quick Breads

Proportions for Batters and Doughs

Pour Batter   1 part liquid to 1 to 1½ parts flour
Drop Batter   1 part liquid to 2 to 2½ parts flour
Soft Dough   1 part liquid to 3 to 3½ parts flour
Stiff Dough   1 part liquid to 4 or more parts flour

In standard cook books in the recipes for all batters and doughs except yeast breads FLOUR unless otherwise specified, means pastry flour. If bread flour is used, about two tablespoons less to the cup must be used, or the mixture will be too stiff.

MIXING BATTERS—GENERAL METHOD

Mix and sift all dry ingredients into a bowl. Beat egg slightly, melt fat, and add to milk. Make a well in the center of the dry ingredients and pour in the liquid ingredients gradually, stirring constantly. When all ingredients are thoroughly blended pour at once into greased pans and bake.

MIXING DOUGHS—GENERAL METHOD

Mix and sift all dry ingredients, cut in cold fat with case knives. When the fat is thoroughly blended, cut in liquid with case knife. The dough is the right consistency for rolling out when it rolls up into a ball without sticking to the edges of the bowl. Roll out on a slightly floured board to the desired thickness and cut.

POPOVERS

1 c flour   1 egg
1 c milk   ¼ t salt

Into a bowl sift flour and salt. Mix egg with milk, and add to flour, stirring to mix and to prevent lumps. Have the gem pans (earthen or iron are best) already greased. Bake at 500° F. for 15 minutes then reduce to 400° F. for 30 minutes. Each cake should have doubled in size and should be dry, crisp and hollow. If not thoroughly baked, they will shrivel and be moist and soft inside.

SWEET MILK GRIDDLE CAKES

1 pt. flour   2 eggs
½ t salt   1½ to 2 c milk
3 t baking powder   2 tb melted shortening
1 tb sugar

Sift together dry ingredients into mixing bowl. Beat eggs until light. Stir eggs and 1 c milk into flour mixture. Add melted butter, beat thoroughly. Then add as much more milk as is needed to make a batter the consistency of thick cream. Beat well before each frying. Use a large griddle uniformly hot. Grease lightly with a bit of fat on fork, leaving just a film of grease. Drop batter from end of spoon, making cakes round and of uniform size. When full of bubbles and before they look dry on top, turn over with cake turner or broad knife. If any portion of batter spatters out on edge, push it immediately up to the cake that there may be no waste and no ragged edges. When they stop puffing they are usually brown and done.

With a good soapstone griddle no greasing will be required.

—From Home Science Cook Book.

SOUR MILK GRIDDLE CAKES

Substitute sour milk or buttermilk for sweet milk in any recipe and use soda in the proportion of 1 t to the pint sour milk. Sour cream may be used if available, in which case a little less soda is used and butter omitted. A little baking powder is sometimes added with the cream and soda, especially if small amount is prepared.

1 c stale bread crumbs may be softened in 1 c boiling water, beaten till smooth, and used as substitute for 2 to 3 eggs. Rice may be used in same manner.

PLAIN MUFFINS

1 pt. flour	1 egg
3½ t baking powder	1 c milk
¼ t salt	1 tb shortening
1 tb sugar	

Sift dry ingredients into mixing bowl. Stir in milk, beating well. Add egg beaten light and lastly, shortening, melted before adding. Mix thoroughly. The shortening may be butter, clarified drippings, suet, bacon fat, etc., or shortening may be omitted, if desired.

Grease muffin tins, fill about two-thirds full. Bake rather quickly in moderately hot oven at 375° F.

GRAHAM OR RYE MUFFINS

In any muffin recipe graham or rye flour may be substituted for equal weight of wheat flour. Often, with these darker flours, molasses is used instead of sugar.

RYE MUFFINS

1¼ c rye flour	¼ c molasses
1¼ c white flour	1¼ c milk
4 t baking powder	1 egg
1 t salt	1 tb shortening, melted

TWIN MOUNTAIN MUFFINS

¼ c fat	¼ t salt
¼ c sugar	2 c flour
1 egg	3 t baking powder
¾ c milk	

Cream fat as for cake, add sugar gradually, add egg beaten well. Sift baking powder with flour and salt and beat into first mixture, alternating with milk. Fill greased muffin tins about two-thirds full and bake in moderate oven, about 25 minutes.

QUICK NUT BREAD

3 c flour	1½ c milk
4½ t baking powder	1 c chopped nuts
1 t salt	¼ c sugar (or none)

Sift well together dry ingredients, reserving a little flour. Add milk, beating mixture thoroughly. Sift flour over chopped nuts, and stir into mixture. Place in greased bread pan. Bake in moderate oven forty-five minutes to one hour.

Chopped raisins, dates, or figs may be substituted for nuts.

BAKING POWDER BISCUIT

2 c flour	1 tb shortening or more
4 t baking powder	2/3 c liquid (milk or water, or
½ t salt	part of each)

Sift flour, baking powder and salt into mixing bowl. Add shortening, which may be lard, butter, clarified drippings, etc. Use two knives for this purpose. Then add liquid gradually, cutting it in. Care must be used in this mixing, more or less liquid being required by different flour. The dough should be stiff enough to roll but not sticky or crumbly. A very little flour should be lightly sifted over the molding board, and the dough tossed about in it with the knife, that the outer surface may be lightly coated with flour to prevent sticking to board or rolling pin. Dough may then be patted out with a knife or rolled out with rolling pin. Keep dough round, not ragged or irregular in shape. Rolling pin should be held lightly and rolled from center outward. Roll to desired thickness, usually ¼ to ¾ inch. Flour biscuit cutter. Bake in quick oven at 400° F.

SODA BISCUIT

Prepare same as baking powder biscuit, substituting sour milk before it is thick and clabbered, or better, buttermilk, for the sweet milk, using ⅓ t soda to each cup milk and making a little stiffer, enough so to knead. Knead 5 minutes, or until smooth. Or use 1 t baking powder to the cup of flour, in addition to the soda. This is especially desirable for the small quantities used in school work.

CORN BREAD OR JOHNNY CAKE

1 c cornmeal	¼ c sugar or molasses
1 c flour	1 egg
½ t salt	1 c sour milk
½ t soda	2 tb melted shortening

Sift together dry ingredients. If molasses is used add it next, rinsing out cup in which it was measured with the sour milk. Beat egg light. Add to mixture, following with milk and fat. Beat well. Bake in one pan 30 to 40 minutes or about 25 minutes in muffin pans. Oven should be moderate, as corn meal burns easily.

MOLASSES GINGERBREAD

2 c flour	¾ c molasses or part each molasses and sugar
½ t salt	
1 t soda	½ c sour milk
1 tb or less ginger	2 tb melted shortening
1 egg	

Sift together dry ingredients. Add egg, well beaten, then other ingredients in order given. Shortening may well be cheaper fat than butter. Beat well. Spread in shallow pan or fill muffin tins two-thirds full. Bake in very moderate oven twenty minutes or more.

BOSTON BROWN BREAD

1 c corn meal	1 c sour milk
1 c rye or graham flour	½ c molasses
½ t salt	½ c raisins, if desired
1 t soda	

Sift together dry ingredients. Mix well with sour milk and molasses. If mixture is too stiff, thin with a little water. If raisins are used, either add to dry mixture before liquid, or reserve out little flour, sift well over raisins and stir in last. Grease baking powder cans or molds, and cover, fill half full with batter. Steam three hours or more, depending on size of mold used. This will make one full sized loaf.

YEAST BREAD

Score Card

EXTERNAL FACTORS—
Shape 5
Size 5
Crust
    Color (even golden brown on all sides).............................. 6
    Smoothness and texture 4

INTERNAL FACTORS—
Depth of Crust...:..... 5
Crumb
    Texture 20
    Elasticity 5
    Moisture 5
    Color 5

FLAVOR 35

Total 100

TEMPERATURE FOR BAKING YEAST BREADS
White bread—430° F. for 30 minutes, then decrease to 380° F.
Rolls—480° F. for 15 minutes.

YEAST EXPERIMENTS
Conditions for the Growth of the Yeast Plant

1. Mix 1 tb of flour, 1 tb sugar, ¾ cake of compressed yeast and 5 tb water. Put 1 tb of the mixture in a test tube and mark "a," fill the tube nearly full of lukewarm water and stand in a warm place for 15 minutes. Examine, noting especially the appearance at the top of the test tube. What kind of substance (gas, liquid, or solid) has been formed by the growth of the yeast plants?

2. Put 1 t of the mixture in a test tube and fill with boiling water. Label "b" and after 15 minutes examine. Is there any change in the contents of the tube? What has happened to the yeast plants?

3. Put 1 t of the mixture in a test tube and fill nearly full of cold water and label it "c." Surround with cracked ice or if the weather is cold place it out doors. After 15 minutes examine. Is there any change in the contents of the tube? Why don't the yeast plants grow?

4. Surround the tube marked "c" with lukewarm water and stand in a warm place. After 15 minutes examine. Are the yeast plants growing? Does freezing kill yeast plants?

5. Mix ⅛ cake yeast with a little lukewarm water. Stand in a warm place and after 15 min. examine. Will yeast grow in water alone?

6. Mix ⅛ cake yeast, 1 tb sugar and a little lukewarm water. Set aside in a warm place so that the yeast plants may grow. Then examine under the microscope. Are there any budding cells? Make a drawing as they appear. Draw at least two practical conclusions from these experiments as to the use and care of yeast for bread making.

—From Greer's "School and Home Cooking."

7. Protein in Flour

Make a stiff dough of 2 tb bread flour and ½ tb water. Knead well and allow to stand for 20 minutes. Then tie dough in cheese cloth, place in a bowl of water, and knead for a few minutes.

Pour a little of the water in a test tube, drain the remainder of the water from the dough. Add more water to the bowl. Again knead the dough under clean water.

Examine the material in the cloth. What color is it? Feel and pull it. Put a little on a plate to dry, and bake some in the oven. Examine after drying and baking. How has it changed in size by heating?

Test the water in the test tube for starch.

Greer—'School and Home Cooking."

YEAST BREAD

1 c liquid	½ tb shortening
1 t salt	¼ to 1 yeast cake
1 t sugar	3 c+flour

Liquid may be milk, or water, or half of each. If milk is used it must be scalded. Skimmed milk may well be used. Melt shortening, which may be butter, lard or other fat, in hot milk. Add salt and sugar. Yeast cake should have been previously broken into 2 tb water to soften and dissolve. When milk has been cooled to about 98° F., or to the temperature we know as "lukewarm," yeast may be stirred in. Gradually, sift in flour, mixing first with spoon. When about half the flour has been added, beat mixture long and thoroughly, until it becomes frothy. Continue adding flour. When too stiff for use of spoon, take knife. Turn on floured board, cover outer surface of dough with flour to prevent stickiness, knead till smooth. To knead, pull dough forward with fingers and push backward with hand. Keep flour between dough and hand, and dough and board. Avoid getting fingers sticky. Place dough in bowl lightly greased, or slightly dampened with water. Cover closely and let rise till double in size. Then repeat kneading process for few moments, shape into loaves WITHOUT ADDING MORE FLOUR, place in greased pan. Cover, let rise till more than double in size. Bake.

Instead of shaping into loaf, dough may be divided into twelve portions and each shaped into roll. Place on greased tin, let rise till more than double in size. Bake in quick oven.

ENTIRE WHEAT OR GRAHAM BREAD

The recipe for yeast bread may be used, substituting entire wheat or graham flour for half or two-thirds of the wheat flour.

PLAIN ROLLS WITH SPONGE

1 c liquid	1 tb shortening
1 t salt	¼ yeast cake or more
1 tb sugar	3+c flour

Follow directions for mixing yeast bread, add 1½ c flour only. Let stand over night, or if less time is to be given, use more yeast. This is the "sponge stage" and when light it will have doubled in bulk and be full of bubbles. Then add about 1½ c more flour. Knead well. Let rise as for bread. Knead again, shape into rolls, let rise. Bake.

TO GLAZE PARKER HOUSE ROLLS OR OTHER FANCY BREADS

1. Brush with melted fat, or milk and sugar (1 tb sugar to ¼ c milk) before baking.
2. When taken from oven, brush with egg, slightly beaten and diluted with 1 tb water or milk. Either yolk or white diluted with water or milk, may be used instead of whole egg.
3. When baked and nearly cool, brush over with confectioner's sugar, moistened with boiling water enough to spread, and flavored.

GERMAN COFFEE BREAD

1 c scalded milk	¼ to 1 yeast cake
¼ c shortening	½ t salt
¼ c sugar	¼ c raisins or currants
1 egg	Flour to mix stiff batter

Mix as sponge for bread, adding egg well beaten, and raisins chopped. Amount of flour used will vary. Mixture should be a drop batter. Beat thoroughly. Scrape side of mixing bowl till clean and free from batter. Cover closely and let rise till very light. Then beat again, add more flour. Mixture should be stiff batter, but not stiff enough to knead. Let rise again, and when light, spread about ½ inch thick in shallow, greased pan. Or, all the flour may be mixed in before set to rise first time and when mixture is light, it may be spread in pan as directed. Bread pan may be used instead of shallow pan, as directed. Let rise in baking pan till very light.

Before baking, brush over with beaten egg and cover with following mixture:

3 tb melted fat	1 t cinnamon
¼ c sugar	3 tb flour

Or, bread may be merely brushed over with melted fat, and sugar and cinnamon mixed and sifted over.

Egg may be omitted in coffee bread, if desired, as may also the raisins or currants. Slices of apples, or peaches, or any preserved fruit, or blanched almonds may be placed on top before baking, instead of sugar and cinnamon. ½ c coffee (liquid) may be substituted for half the milk.

Coffee bread may be made from sponge for plain bread. Let rise and take out part. Before adding more flour, beat in shortening, sugar, egg and fruit.

Cheese and Milk Dishes

MILK EXPERIMENTS

1. Examine a milk bottle obtained from a reliable dealer.
    a   Read the statements on the cap.
    b   Of what significance are they?
    c   What are the two layers in the bottle?
    d   Why is the yellow layer at the top?
2. Examine with a microscope a tiny drop of cream.
    a   Make a drawing of the fat droplets.
3. Prepare 4 junket custards, using 1 c sweet milk and ¼ junket tablet dissolved in ¾ tb cold water in each instance. Proceed as follows:
    a   Add dissolved junket tablet to cold milk.
    b   Add dissolved junket tablet to warm milk.
    c   Add dissolved junket tablet to milk and boil 1 minute.
    d   Add dissolved junket tablet to cold milk.
  Put a, b, and c in room temperature. Put d in the refrigerator.
    e   Compare results at the end of 10 minutes.
    f   Which method has proven most satisfactory?
    g   Why?
    h   What is junket?

COTTAGE CHEESE I

2 c whole milk	1 t butter
⅛ t salt	2 tb cream

Let milk stand in warm place (90° to 99° F.), until it curdles. Drain through cheese cloth placed over colander; press until whey ceases to separate; add butter and cream, and shape into balls or cakes, with spatulas. Or, use sour milk and heat it gently in double boiler until the curd forms, then proceed as above.

COTTAGE CHEESE II

2 c whole milk	2 tb cream

½ junket tablet dissolved in 2 t lukewarm water

Heat milk until lukewarm; add rennet and let stand until firm; then cut into dice with a knife and drain in cheese cloth placed over colander; press under weight until whey no longer can be pressed out; season with salt; moisten with cream and form into balls. Minced onion, chives, or caraway seed are seasonings that may be added to cottage cheese.

CHEESE FONDUE

1 c stale bread crumbs	1 tb fat
1 c or ¼ lb. cheese (cut fine)	½ t salt
1 c milk	⅛ t mustard
2 eggs	⅛ t paprika

Mix bread, milk and cheese in a double boiler. When cheese is melted, add eggs, beaten until well mixed, and seasonings. Cook until thick and perfectly smooth.

The same mixture may be prepared by placing bread and cheese in layers, in oiled pudding dish, and pouring over it milk, mixed

EGGS

1. Have water boiling in sauce pan when egg is put in, boil rapidly for 3 minutes.
2. Put an egg in water at 80° C., cover and let stand for 10 minutes.
3. Boil an egg for 10 minutes.
4. Boil an egg for 20 minutes.
5. Put an egg in water at 80° C., cover and let stand for 45 minutes.
6. Put an egg in water at the boiling point, cover and let stand for 45 minutes.
   —Taken from "Laboratory Manual of Foods and Cookery" by Matteson & Newlands.
7. Place a teaspoonful of egg white in a test tube. Insert a thermometer in the test tube and place the test tube in a sauce pan of water. Heat the water gradually and note the temperature at which coagulation first appears and when coagulation is complete. Has the water in the sauce pan reached the boiling point?
8. Break an egg and measure the yolk, beat with Dover egg beater and measure again. Any change?
9. Measure the white of an egg, beat with Dover egg beater and measure again. Result?
10. Measure the white of an egg and beat with wire egg whisk, measure again. Result? Compare with 9. Conclusions.
11. Break an egg, measure, beat with Dover egg beater and measure again. Result?
12. Weigh eggs in the shell to see how many medium sized eggs in a pound and how many small eggs in a pound.
13. Break an egg and cook it in boiling water until the white is set.
14. Break an egg and cook it in water at the simmering point until white is set. Compare results in 13 and 14.

COOKED EGGS

Put eggs in saucepan of cold water and heat. By the time water boils, the eggs will be ready to eat. Or, put eggs in boiling water and place dish containing them where water will keep hot, but cannot boil. In five minutes, the white will be soft and jelly-like. In ten minutes the yolk will begin to be firm. Water at 180° F. is about right for cooking eggs. For hard eggs, cook in water of 180° F. for half an hour, or longer.
—Home Science Cook Book.

POACHED EGGS

Oil the inside of a shallow pan, and of as many muffin rings as eggs to be poached. Put muffin rings into pan and pour over them enough boiling, salted water to cover eggs, allowing 1 t salt to 1 pint of water. Place pan of water where it will keep hot, but not boil. Break eggs, one at a time, carefully into a cup and slip gently into muffin rings. The yolk must not be broken, and the water must not boil. As the white begins to coagulate, dip some of

with egg and seasoning; then baking till firm, in moderate oven, testing with knife, as for all custard mixtures.

Macaroni, rice, or other cooked cereal may be substituted for bread crumbs. More or less cheese may be used. One egg will often be sufficient, or three may be preferred. Whites and yolks may be separated, and whites stiffly beaten, folded in last. Then bake in oiled pudding dish.

CHEESE SOUFFLE

1 c white sauce II*	½ t salt
1 c chopped cheese	spk cayenne
3 eggs	¼ t soda

In hot, white sauce, melt cheese, cut very fine. Let stand till cool. Add yolks, beaten till light, also soda and seasonings. Fold in stiffly beaten egg whites. Turn into buttered baking dish. Place in pan of warm water and bake in moderate oven, till firm and well puffed up. Serve immediately.

RAREBIT

½ c milk or cream	½ t salt
2 c or ½ lb. cheese	spk cayenne
2 tb fat	¼ t soda
2 eggs	

Put milk and grated cheese in upper part of double boiler, or blazer of chafing dish. When cheese is melted, add fat. Pour this mixture over eggs, slightly beaten; then return to double boiler. Add soda and seasoning. Stir constantly, and cook until smooth and thick. Serve at once, over slices of toast, or hot crisp crackers.

* See page — for directions.

ESCALLOPED CHEESE

2 qts. bread, cut in one-half inch cubes	1 qt. medium white sauce*
	1 pt. grated cheese

Arrange in baking dish in alternate layers with cheese on top. Bake in very moderate oven about 45 minutes.

MACARONI WITH CHEESE

1 c macaroni	¼ c chopped or grated cheese
1 c white sauce*	buttered crumbs

Break macaroni into pieces one inch long. Drop slowly into two quarts of boiling salted water and cook till tender (20 to 40 minutes), drain in a colander. Hot water poured over it will wash off some of surplus starch, and separate parts. Stir cheese into hot well seasoned white sauce and mix with macaroni, or, put macaroni and sauce in buttered baking dish in layers, sprinkle buttered crumbs on top and brown well in hot oven.

Chopped green peppers may be added for additional flavor.

* See page — for directions.

hot water over eggs with spoon, until film forms over yolks. When eggs are jelly-like, remove muffin rings; gently lift eggs with a skimmer, drain, and place on slices of hot buttered toast. The eggs may be poached without using muffin rings, but require trimming to give edges a good shape.

Milk, stock, tomato sauce,* or gravy may be substituted for water and served over the toast. Grated cheese, minced chives, or chopped meat may be sprinkled over toast, before eggs are placed on it, or may be lightly sprinkled over eggs. Poached eggs may be served on fish balls, meat cakes, potato cakes, mound of spinach, or other vegetables.

SCRAMBLED EGGS

6 eggs
6 tb milk
3 tb fat

⅛ t pepper
½ t salt

The general rule is to use 1 tb milk and ½ tb butter for each egg.

Beat eggs slightly to mix whites and yolks, add salt, pepper and milk. Put fat into hot omelet pan. When melted, pour in the mixture. Cook slowly at a low temperature, until creamy consistency, lifting from bottom of pan, with spatula, as it thickens. Do not stir, but leave in rather large masses. Serve on hot, buttered toast. Or, scrambled eggs may be prepared by placing butter and milk and seasoning in omelet pan; when hot drop eggs into this mixture. Have slow fire. Lift eggs from pan with spatula, folding over and over, till thickened.

Minced onion, chives, chopped ham, peppers, or mushrooms may be stirred in.

BAKED EGGS

Oil ramekins, or egg shirrers, or muffin tins. Break an egg into each and bake in slow oven until firm. Dishes may be lined with crumbs or chopped ham, cheese, or parsley, before putting in eggs. Thick slices of toast (about ¾ to 1 inch) cut in squares or rounds, may be slightly hollowed out in center, a bit of butter and an egg placed on each, and baked in oven.

CREAMED EGGS

Use white sauce* following the usual rule of half as much sauce as vegetable or meat.

Cut eggs in halves or quarters, and add to white sauce, or pour sauce over eggs, on shallow dish. 1 tb curry may be used for each cup of white sauce, and curried eggs prepared. In the same way eggs may be served in tomato sauce. Serve over toast.

SCALLOPED EGGS

Chop hard cooked eggs. Use half as much white sauce* as egg. Place in layers in oiled baking dish, covering with buttered crumbs. Brown in oven.

TO BUTTER CRUMBS

Crumb the soft part of stale bread by rubbing two slices together, or if bread is thoroughly dry, put through meat grinder. Melt 1½ tb butter for each cup crumbs. Stir crumbs into butter lightly with fork. Seasoning may be added.

---

* See page 94 for directions.

COLDENROD EGGS

Use two or three hard cooked eggs to each cup of medium white sauce*. Separate the yolks from the whites, chop the whites fine and add to the white sauce. Pour the white sauce over slices of toast and sprinkle the yolks which have been put through a ricer or strainer on top. Sprinkle with parsley.

SAUTEED EGGS

Use ½ tb fat (bacon or ham fat, clarified beef drippings, or vegetable oil), for each egg. Melt fat in omelet pan. When hot, slip in egg, and let cook over low fire, till jelly-like. They may be turned, if desired. Edges of eggs should not become brown or crisp. Or, a quantity of fat may be used, bacon or ham fat being preferable. Slip egg into fat, and with spoon dip fat over egg. Remove with skimmer.

FRENCH OMELET

6 eggs	¼ t pepper
6 tb liquid	3 tb fat
½ t salt	

The general rule is for each egg, use 1 tb liquid, ½ tb butter. Season to taste.

Break eggs into bowl, beat slightly to mix, or until they can be taken up on spoon; add seasonings and liquid, which may be cold water, milk, or stock. Have ready a smooth, hot omelet pan, (light weight, small pan is best) in which fat has been melted. Shake the pan so that every part is coated with fat. Pour beaten eggs into pan. As egg cooks, shake pan lightly, and with fork or spatula, gently lift egg. Tip pan, so that some of uncooked portion can run to side. When puffed, creamy, and lightly browned on the bottom, take pan in left hand, tilting pan downward. With knife, loosen edge of omelet from pan. Make slight cut in middle at each side, at right angles to the handle of the pan, but not entirely through the omelet. Fold quickly, and turn on to a hot plate, from which it is to be served, at once.

From ¼ to ½ c of any meat or vegetable may be minced and seasoned and either mixed with omelet before cooking or folded into it. If folded in, material should be hot. Minced ham, bacon, chopped cheese, or oysters, mushrooms, parsley, cooked asparagus, celery, cauliflower, spinach, peppers, or jelly may be so used.

By the use of more yolks than whites, a creamier omelet is obtained.

PUFFY OMELET OR OMELET SOUFFLE

6 egg whites	½ t salt
6 egg yolks	⅛ t pepper
6 tb milk	3 tb fat

Beat whites of eggs stiff and dry. Beat egg yolks until light lemon color; add milk and seasonings, and beat again to mix thoroughly. Fold in, carefully, the beaten whites, using a spatula; or yolks may be poured over whites gradually, beating them in. Pour into hot omelet pan, in which fat has been melted, and well coated over entire surface. Shake pan gently. Let cook till lower side is dry, and delicately colored. Remove quickly, to a moderately hot oven, to dry upper surface, not to brown it; or omelet pan may be held under low gas flame. When the upper side does not cling to spatula, and appears dry, take from oven, fold as directed in "French Omelet." Turn onto hot platter, and serve at once.

---

* See page 94 for directions.

CREAMY OMELET

6 eggs	¼ t pepper
1¼ c white sauce II*	3 tb fat
1 t salt	

Make either French or puffy omelet using white sauce instead of water. Pour another half cup white sauce around it before serving, after it has been placed on a hot platter.

---

* See page 94 for directions.

SALMON LOAF

½ to 1 can salmon	1 t salt
2 eggs	⅓ t pepper
½ c milk	1 t lemon juice
1 c stale crumbs	1 t or more chopped parsley

Remove skin and bone of salmon. Mince fish with silver fork and add eggs, well beaten. Add crumbs, buttered if desired, and seasoning. Mix well. Put in a greased mold, cover and steam or bake 1 hour. Hard cooked egg, slices of pickle, or olives may be imbedded in fish mold. Left-overs of baked fish and stuffing may be utilized. Serve hot with white sauce* or the following:

EGG SAUCE (for Fish)

1/3 c fat	⅓ t pepper
3 tb flour	2 yolks
1½ c hot water	1 tb lemon juice
½ t salt	

Melt one-half the butter, add flour and seasoning, and pour gradually on hot water. Boil 5 minutes, add remaining butter. Pour on the beaten yolks, add lemon juice.

SALMON BOX

Line a bread pan slightly oiled with warmed steamed rice. Fill center with cold salmon, flaked and seasoned with salt, pepper, and slight grating of nutmeg. Cover with rice and steam or bake one hour. Turn on a hot platter for serving and pour around an egg sauce.

SCALLOPED TUNA FISH

3 c bread cubes	1 small onion
1½ c white sauce*	4 tb fat
1 small, or ½ large can fish	

Slice and brown onion in the fat. Remove onion, put bread cubes into same fat and brown lightly. Arrange cubes and sauce in alternate layers in greased baking dish, bake about one-half hour in moderate oven.

Any kind of canned or left-over fish could be used. Instead of bread, any kind of creamed vegetables, or vegetables may be alternated with the fish.

CODFISH BALLS OR CODFISH PUFF

1 c salt codfish	1 tb fat
2 c potatoes	⅓ t pepper
1 egg	

Wash fish in cold water and pull into small pieces, keeping fish in water while doing so. Wash and pare the potatoes and cut into pieces. Cook the fish and potatoes together in boiling water until the potatoes are tender, then drain and shake over the fire until dry; mash, and beat thoroughly with a wire potato masher. Add the fat, and pepper and salt if needed. Cool slightly, then add beaten egg, and beat until light. Take up mixture in a spoon, mold slightly

---

* See page 94 for directions.

54

FISH

PREPARATION OF FRESH FISH FOR COOKERY

Cover board or table with newspaper before laying fish down. Remove scales by scraping a dull knife from tail to head, snapping scales off. Rinse knife in water occasionally. Wet hands before touching fish, and odor will come off more easily. Dip hands in salt so that fish will not slip, and hold by tail. If inner organs have not been removed in market, make a lengthwise incision on the underneath side, and draw or scrape them out carefully, so that membrane which lines cavity is not broken. Remove head if desired; if left on, cut out eyes. Remove fins with scissors. Wash inside and out in salted water. Sprinkle fish with salt if to be kept over night. Handle fish carefully when cooking, as flesh falls apart easily, and have all utensils well greased as skin sticks readily when heated. When fish is cooked the flesh separates from the bone.

STUFFED AND BAKED FISH

Clean fish, sprinkle with salt, and fill with stuffing, sew or skewer the edges together. Cut gashes on each side across the fish, and put strips of salt pork into them. Fold a piece of well greased paper about tail. Grease the baking pan and line it with greased paper. Place the fish upon it, dredge with flour, salt, and pepper, and lay salt pork strips about it. Place in a hot oven. Baste every 10 minutes. Cook 15 minutes to the pound, and 15 minutes over. Add water to pan if necessary.

STUFFING FOR FISH

2 c stale bread or cracker crumbs	1 t onion juice
½ t salt	1 t chopped parsley or green pepper
⅛ t pepper	1 t capers
cayenne	¼ c beef drippings

Mix in order given. Instead of capers a teaspoon lemon juice, or vinegar, or of chopped pickle may be used. Less fat may be used and some water used to moisten dressing.

BROILED FISH

Clean fish, cut into pieces and lay on a well greased broiler. If fish is dry, rub it with melted fat before placing on broiler. Sear the flesh side first, then turn every 10 seconds. The length of time for cooking depends on the thickness of the fish, 20 to 30 minutes. Season with butter, salt, and pepper.

FRIED FISH

Clean fish, cut in fillets, or sections of uniform thickness. Wipe dry, cover with well seasoned corn meal and flour (mixed in equal parts), or fine bread crumbs, and egg. Cook in deep fat or saute in salt pork fat. Drain on absorbent paper.

with a knife, and slip into deep hot fat*. Fry until brown, about 1 minute. Drain on absorbent paper.

Mixture for codfish balls may be served hot, without frying, or turned into a buttered baking dish and browned in the oven and served as a baked dish, or shaped into flat cakes and sauteed in frying pan. To make codfish puff, prepare in same manner, only use two well beaten eggs. Cook like an omelet.

FRIED OYSTERS

Select large oysters, remove pieces of shell, wash and wipe dry. Roll in well seasoned, dry, bread crumbs, which have been sifted. Dip in egg (beaten with 1 tb water or oyster juice), and again in the crumbs. Fry in deep fat* 1 minute. Drain on absorbent paper. Or, saute in frying pan, using one tablespoon fat to cup of oysters.

SCALLOPED OYSTERS

1 qt. oysters	cayenne
2 c crumbs	6 tb fat
½ t salt	½ c liquid

Wash oysters with ¾ c cold water in colander and remove pieces of shell. Strain the juice. Melt fat, add crumbs and seasoning. Line the bottom of a greased baking dish with ¼ the crumbs then add ½ the oysters. Add ¼ more crumbs, and remainder of oysters and liquid, which may be liquid from oysters, or milk. Cover with buttered crumbs**. Bake in a moderate oven 30 to 40 minutes. A large shallow pan is always preferable to a deep baking pan.

OYSTER STEW

1 qt. oysters	½ tb salt
1 qt. milk	⅛ tb pepper
¼ c fat	

Clean the oysters by placing in colander and pouring over them ¾ c cold water. Pick over carefully, removing any bits of shell that adhere. Reserve liquid, heat to boiling point, strain through double cheese cloth over wire strainer. Add oysters, cook until edges begin to curl. Add oysters and liquor to hot, scalded milk; add fat and seasoning. Serve at once.

Paprika, celery salt, onion juice, parsley or mace may be used as additional seasoning, if desired.

For oyster soup, thicken the milk, using ½ tb flour for each cup of milk. Prepare as for white sauce. Two egg yolks may be beaten and added to milk just before serving, or use water instead of milk and add 1 c cream.

---

* See page 114 for directions.　** See page 48 for directions.

MEATS

CUTS OF BEEF
Hind Quarter

ROUND—
  Rump.
    1. Rump.
  Round: Rump and shank off.
    2.-14. Round steaks inclusive.
    15. Knuckle soup bone.
    16. Pot Roast.
  Hind Shank.
    17.-18 Soup bones.
    19. Hock soup bones.
LOIN—
  (counting from upper part down.)
  First Cut—Butt-end sirloin steak.
  Second Cut—Wedge-bone sirloin steak.
  Third and Fourth—Round-bone sirloin steak.
  Fifth and Sixth—Double-bone sirloin steak.
  Seventh—Hip-bone sirloin steak.
  Eighth—Hip-bone porterhouse steak.
  Next seven cuts—Regular porterhouse steak.
  Last three cuts—Club steaks.
FLANK—
  1. Flank.
  2. Stew.

Fore Quarter

RIB—
  1. 11 and 12 rib roast.
  2. 9 and 10th rib roast.
  3. 8 and 8th rib roast.
  4. 6th rib roast.
CHUCK—
  1. 5th rib roast.
  Second to Ninth cuts inclusive—Chuck steaks.
  10.-13. Pot roasts.
  14. Clod.
  15. Neck.
PLATE—
  1. Brisket.
  2. Navel.
  3.-4. Rib ends.
FORE SHANK—
  1. Stew.
  2. Knuckle soup bone.
  3.-6. Soup bones.

SOUP STOCK

2 lbs. meat and bone	1 t sweet herbs
2 qt. cold water	1 small bay leaf
½ c minced onion	1 sprig parsley
½ c carrot	1 piece celery root
½ c turnip	4 cloves
6 peppercorns	

Cheap cuts of meat, shin, or neck, joints, and small scraps of meat such as the flank end of steak, or left overs and bones of roasts, may be used for soup stock. Beef, veal or chicken are most commonly used. Cut the meat into small pieces and wipe clean. In general, use twice as much meat as bone, and for each pound of meat and bone, use about one quart of water. Put the meat and bone into cold salted water, and if possible, let soak for an hour. Then place over low fire and simmer gently about three hours. If vegetables are to be used for seasoning add now, allowing from half cup to cup of mixed vegetables for each pound of meat used. These vegetables may be onion, carrot, turnip, peppers, celery or cabbage, using such combinations as are desired. Mixed herbs and spices may be tied in cheese cloth and added, and left in simmering soup as long as desired. Pepper corns, cloves, bay leaf, parsley, celery salt, mace, thyme, and marjorum, may be used as desired.

After vegetables and seasonings are added, cook two hours or more. If clear soup is desired, the froth should be skimmed from stock as it rises, otherwise it is not necessary. For clear soup, strain, cool. Then remove cold fat by dipping it off with spoon, and then removing finer particles by means of piece of cheese cloth dipped in ice water, or with piece of ice folded within cheese cloth.

It is usually well, in preparing soup stock, to prepare larger quantity at a time. By placing in sterilized jars, in cool place, it may be kept several days.

After stock has been strained and cooled, the lower portion will be found to be thicker and contain the largest amount of solid and nutritive material. Ofter this may be used for thick soup or sauces, while the upper part, with less waste, may be used for clear soups.

TO CLEAR SOUP

Use 1 egg white to each quart of cold stock. Beat egg slightly, and add to stock. Heat gradually till near the boiling point, stirring all the time. Cook gently for fifteen minutes. Remove to back of range and add ¼ c cold water. Let stand few minutes, then strain through cheese cloth placed over strainer. Heat, add any further seasoning desired.

PAN BROILED STEAK

Trim fat from steak, also part of bone, if desired. Wipe with damp cloth. Heat frying pan till very hot, or until blue smoke arises. Rub surface of pan with little fat. Place steak in pan, searing it quickly, first one side, then on the other. Be careful in turning, not to pierce with fork. After both sides are seared, reduce heat under the pan and cook steak more slowly, turning every 10 seconds. Stand on edge to brown fat. Keep pan free from fat. Steak is done rare, when well browned, and puffy. If one inch thick, this will take about 8 minutes. If desired well done, it will require 12 to 15 minutes or more.

OVEN BROILED STEAK

For gas stove, use oven broiler. Heat till very hot. Brush broiler with melted fat. Place steak near blaze until seared and browned, then place farther from blaze and cook slowly, turning frequently. If coal or wood range is used, broil steak over coal, on wire broiler, following same directions.

POT ROAST OF BEEF—GRAVY

Nearly any of the tough meats may be used. The rump or lower part of the round is preferable. Wipe meat, sear in hot frying pan, or in the kettle used for roasting. Lard outer surface if meat is lean, a few slices of salt pork may be cooked with meat. Place in kettle, add ½ c boiling water to 2 lbs. meat, and cover tightly. Cook slowly until meat is very tender and well browned, adding only enough water to prevent burning. Season when nearly done. Serve with brown gravy made with liquid left in the pan. Instead of water, strained tomatoes may be used with pot roast. For seasoning, in addition to salt and pepper, a bit of bay leaf, parsley, a few cloves, or slices of carrot may be cooked with the roast.

GRAVY

To each cup of liquid, add, gradually, 2 tb of flour mixed till smooth, with an equal quantity of cold water. Cook as white sauce. Strain.

BEEF STEW

2 lbs. beef	1 qt. stock or water
1 onion	6 potatoes
½ c carrot	1 t salt
¼ c turnip	¼ t pepper

Cut beef into 2 inch cubes. Reserve the tenderest pieces of meat. Place the tougher portions and bone into cold water or stock. Put over slow fire and heat gradually to boiling point. Dredge reserved meat with flour, and saute in marrow, drippings, or pork fat, and add to stew. Let simmer about two hours. In same frying pan, brown onion, cut in slices, and turnip and carrot, diced. Cook until meat and vegetables are nearly done, then remove bones, skim off fat and add potatoes which have been parboiled ten minutes and drained. Season. Add boiling water if needed. Ten minutes before potatoes are done, add dumplings. Thicken gravy after removing meat, vegetables and dumplings.

½ c rice may be added 10 minutes before potatoes are put in, if desired. 1 pt. strained tomatoes may be substituted for part of water.

Left over roast beef or steak may be utilized for stew. In this case, vegetables may be put on with the meat. Mutton, lamb, or veal may be used in same way. Bones should be included for sake of juices and flavor. Gravy may be used for stock. Sweet herbs, spices, raisins, may be added in the way of flavor, if variety is desired.

DUMPLINGS

	½ t salt
2 c flour	1 c milk or water
4 t baking powder	

Sift dry ingredients together in mixing bowl. Mix to drop batter with liquid. Drop from spoon into boiling liquid, being careful that there is plenty of water and no possibility of boiling dry. Cover closely and cook undisturbed, and rapidly, for from ten to twenty minutes, depending on size of dumplings.

FLANK OR ROUND STEAK, STUFFED AND ROLLED

1 lb. top round, or flank   1 onion sliced
   ½ in. thick   ¼ c carrot cubed
2 or 3 small slices suet   1 c boiling water or stock

STUFFING

1 c crumbs   2 tb chopped celery
2 tb butter (melted)   ½ t salt
2 tb parsley   ⅛ t paprika
½ t onion juice

Trim edges of steak, spread over it stuffing, roll and tie it, and lay it on onion and carrot in pan with suet on top. Pour the water or stock into pan, cook closely covered for 20 minutes or more in a hot oven, then uncover and cook 30 minutes longer. Serve with brown gravy made from drippings in pan.

BEEF LOAF

2 lbs. beef   1 tb lemon juice, if desired
¼ lb. fat salt pork   ½ c dry crumbs
2 t salt   ¼ c milk
½ t pepper   2 eggs
1 tb chopped parsley   1 onion

Select lean beef, remove skin and membrane, chop fine with salt pork. Add crumbs, seasoning. Brown minced onion in little fat, before adding. Beat eggs slightly, add with milk, mix up well. Pack in mold, such as coffee or baking powder tin, cover tightly and steam for two hours or longer, then brown in oven, basting with melted fat. Or, pack in bread pan, smooth evenly on top and bake in slow oven two hours or more, basting frequently. Or, meat may be shaped into loaf in roaster and baked in oven. May be served hot, with brown gravy or tomato sauce,* or may be used cold. Veal or mutton may be substituted for beef.

VEAL CUTLETS

2½ lbs. veal (from round)   fine bread crumbs
salt   1 egg
pepper   1 tb water
4 tb drippings

Wipe meat and cut into pieces for individual serving, removing bone, skin and tough membranes. Skewer small pieces of meat together with wooden tooth picks. Beat egg and water, so that white is well broken but not light. Roll in sifted, seasoned bread crumbs, dip in egg (using two knives, or knife and fork to handle), then roll in crumbs again. Melt fat in frying pan. When hot, brown cutlets quickly on both sides. Pour tomato sauce* over cutlets, cover, then cook at low temperature for 1 hour or until tender, turning occasionally. Cutlets may be browned in deep fat, in which case, transfer to sauce pan to finish cooking.

SAUCE FOR CUTLETS

2 tb fat   1 pt. stock, water, or strained to-
¼ c flour   mato juice
½ t salt   2 tb chopped parsley, or lemon
1 t Worcestershire   juice, or horseradish
⅛ t pepper

---

* See page 94 for directions.

66

CASSEROLE OF MUTTON

Wipe two and a half pounds mutton or lamb cut from neck. Trim off outer skin and surplus fat. Put in hot frying pan, and turn frequently until seared, and browned on both sides. Brush over with melted butter, or beef drippings. Season with salt and pepper, and bake in casserole dish in slow oven until tender, about an hour or more. Cut carrot strips, and saute in one tablespoon bacon fat or beef drippings, to which has been added one tablespoon finely chopped onion. Add to mutton with one cup diced potato or potato balls, two cups thin brown or tomato sauce. Season to taste. Cook until vegetables are tender, then add about a dozen small onions cooked until tender, then drained and sauteed in butter to which is added a tablespoon sugar. Onions need not be sauteed unless they are desired glazed. Turnips as well as carrots may be added. Parsley and other herbs may be added for seasoning. The vegetables may be cut in fancy shapes with vegetable cutter. Serve from casserole dish. Leftover mutton or lamb from roast may be utilized in this way.

MUTTON CHOPS

Wipe with wet cloth, remove skin and surplus fat. If desired, rib chops may have meat trimmed down from bone two inches, forming "French" chop; or meat may be cut from all the bone, rolled and skewered with toothpicks. Chops may be oven broiled or pan broiled. Follow directions as for broiling steak. Stand them up on the fat edge to brown the fat, without overcooking the meat. Time for cooking will depend on thickness of chop, and whether it is to be served rare or well done. In general, five minutes for rare chops one inch thick, eight minutes for medium, and twelve to fifteen for well done. Drain on absorbent paper. Serve hot.

ROAST PORK

Wipe pork, sprinkle with salt and pepper, place on rack in dripping pan or roaster, and dredge meat and bottom of pan with flour. Place in moderate oven and roast three or four hours, basting every fifteen minutes with fat in pan. For roast pork, the usual rule is twenty-five minutes to the pound. Make gravy, using same proportions as white sauce.

BROILED HAM

Soak thin slices of ham, from which rind has been trimmed, one hour in lukewarm water. Drain, wipe and broil about five minutes.

BACON

Place thin slices of bacon (from which the rind has been removed) closely together on a fine wire broiler; place broiler over dripping pan, or in oven broiler, and bake in a hot oven until bacon is crisp and brown, turning once. Drain on absorbent paper. Save fat for frying purposes. Bacon may be put in hot frying pan and fried till crisp and brown, turning once. It is usually well to drain off part of the fat during the frying.

CREAMED DRIED BEEF

Use one-half cup of finely divided dried beef to one pint of medium white sauce*. It is best to soak the beef in lukewarm water or bring it to the boil in water, draining and then adding to the white sauce to remove some of the salt.

---

* See page 94 for directions.

LEFT OVER MEATS—GENERAL DIRECTIONS

Almost any left over meat may be combined with other foods, well seasoned, and be made up into very palatable dishes. Beef, veal, mutton, lamb, chicken, and ham are all desirable and may be combined. Fish may be substituted for meat in many recipes.

1. Trim off carefully all non-edible parts.
2. Cut or chop meat in fine pieces of uniform size. Do not mash.
3. Since meat is cooked, protect from direct heat by sauce, crumbs, potatoes, etc.
4. Sauce should be thoroughly cooked before adding meat.
5. Season rather highly. Sweet herbs, onions, celery salt, paprika, curry, or tobasco may be used.
6. In general, when sauce or gravy are used, take half as much sauce as meat and vegetable combined.
7. By substituting rice, or other cereal, or macaroni, for potato more variation is offered.

MEAT CROQUETTES

2 c chopped cooked meat   ½ t salt
1 to 2 c white sauce IV*   ⅛ t pepper

In general, use equal amounts of white sauce and meat. Less will be needed if meat is freshly cooked, or if canned meat is used. If very dry, more sauce may be used. Meat should be chopped fine, seasoned rather highly, then moistened with sauce as soft as can be handled. Let chill thoroughly on flat dish, then divide evenly into separate portions, allowing 2 tb for each croquette. Shape into balls, cylinders, cones, or any desired shape. Roll and sift dry crumbs, beat egg with 1 tb water. Roll croquettes in crumbs, dip in egg, again roll in crumbs, and fry in deep fat,** till light brown in color. Drain on soft paper. They may be served with sauce.

Any meat or combination of meats may be used. Fish, eggs, and macaroni may be used in same way. Seasoning may be onion, parsley, celery salt. Lemon juice combines well with fish or chicken.

CASSEROLE OF RICE AND MEAT

2 c chopped cooked meat   1 tb chopped parsley
1 t salt   1 egg
¼ t pepper   ¼ c fine crumbs
¼ t onion juice   4 c cooked rice

Season the meat, mixed with crumbs and beaten egg, and add enough meat stock or boiling water to make mixture pack easily. Line a greased mold, or baking pan, with 2 or 3 c rice. Pack rice well and fill with meat, cover with the remainder of the rice, cover tightly, and steam or bake about 45 minutes. Remove from mold. Serve with tomato sauce.**

SHEPHERD'S PIE OR SCALLOPED MEAT

2 c chopped cooked meat   ¼ t pepper
2 c mashed potato   ¼ t paprika
2 c left over gravy   1 t onion juice
1 t salt   1 or 2 tb fat
It is unnecessary to follow above proportions. Use available

---

* See page 94 for directions.   ** See page 114 for directions.

amounts of meat and potato, and gravy, and season to taste. Line bottom of buttered baking dish with well beaten mashed potato, (either hot or left over). Add thick layer of meat and gravy, then layer of potato, until dish is full. Make the top crust of potato. Dot with bits of fat. Or, meat and gravy may be placed in lower part of baking dish with single thick layer of mashed potato for the crust. Stiffly beaten egg white may be folded into mashed potatoes before adding to meat, if desired. Bake in hot oven till potatoes are brown, or if cold potatoes have been used, till thoroughly heated and browned.

Crumbs, macaroni, rice, or left over cereal of any kind may be substituted for potatoes.

MINCED MEAT ON TOAST

Use any meat, heating in gravy, white sauce,* or tomato sauce. Add butter, season well, and serve on hot toast.

HASH

1 to 2 c chopped meat	1 t minced onion or celery
2 c chopped potato	3 to 4 tb fat
1 t salt	milk, water, or stock to moisten
¼ t pepper	

Any available left over meat may be used, taking about equal parts of meat and potato. Chop meat first, then add potato and chop together. Season. Melt fat (1 tb to each cup of hash) in frying pan, spread hash in evenly and cook slowly for 20 minutes. Shake the pan occasionally to prevent sticking. Roll or fold like an omelet without breaking browned crust. The hash may be put in a buttered pan and baked in the oven.

—From Home Science Cook Book.

---

* See page 94 for directions.

POULTRY

TO CLEAN AND CUT UP FOWL

1. Remove pin feathers, using small pointed knife and pulling feathers with the direction of the growth of the feather, to avoid breaking skin.
2. Singe to remove long hairs, by holding over flame from gas, alcohol or burning paper.
3. Cut off head, using heavy, sharp knife or cleaver.
4. Remove feet and oil gland.
5. Cut off legs, following the natural division of the muscles.
6. Separate at middle joint into drum stick and second joint, by cutting through flesh and unjointing.
7. Cut off wings and separate at middle joint.
8. Separate body by cutting carefully between breast and back through ends of ribs on each side.
9. Disjoint neck from breast.
10. Separate neck piece from end of back, and carefully remove entrails lying in back.
11. Remove kidneys and lungs.
12. Separate breast bone, or "wish bone," with the meat that is on it from the breast.
13. Cut breast across into two pieces with cleaver. If large, it may be further divided.
14. Wash carefully.
15. Prepare giblets as for roast.

STEWED FOWL

After cleaning and cutting up fowl, cover pieces with boiling water, and cook rapidly 15 minutes, then add 1 tb salt, and cook at a low temperature until tender, 1½ hours or more. Add dumplings, if desired. Thicken gravy before serving.

FRICASEED FOWL

Before putting on to stew, dredge fowl with flour and brown well in hot fat. Proceed as for stew, thickening stock as for gravy. Egg yolks may be used for part of thickening, if desired. Chopped parsley, celery, or celery salt, or green pepper may be used for seasoning, if desired.

To arrange bird on platter, lay neck, breast and back in center, in order. On the sides of the breast, lay cut of wings, on the sides of the back lay drum sticks and second joints. Lay giblets between wings and second joints.

POULTRY—TO DRESS AND CLEAN

1. Remove pin feathers.
2. Singe over flame.
3. Cut off head.
4. Turn back skin from neck, and cut off neck close to top of breast. Avoid cutting skin.
5. Place first two fingers under skin of breast, loosen and break membranes attaching wind pipe and crop. Withdraw them. If necessary to cut skin, cut on back.

6. Cut through skin around legs, half inch below the joint. Be careful not to cut through tendons. With skewer, remove tendons. In all but very young birds, each must be removed separately.

7. Make incision through skin at end of breast bone, or under one of the legs. Make only small opening.

8. Insert first two fingers and pass them around close to body, between body and internal organs, at first, close to breast bone, and then beyond liver and heart.

9. After organs are loosened, take hold of gizzard and draw out gently. Rest will follow. Avoid breaking gall bladder, which lies under liver.

10. Cut away anal cavity.

11. The lung and kidneys, lying in the hollows of the back bone must be removed separately and very carefully.

12. Cut out oil sac.

13. Cut gall bladder away from liver.

14. Press heart to extract blood.

15. Remove outer coat of gizzard by cutting through muscular coat to inner lining. Lining membrane must not be cut. Hold in two hands, with the thumbs on each side of incision and pull muscular coat from inner sac.

16. Wash fowl thoroughly inside and out, with cold water containing little soda or charcoal. Wipe. Wash giblets.

ROAST FOWL

After fowl has been dressed and cleaned, fill with stuffing, truss securely in compact shape, and lay on its back in roasting pan. Dredge with flour, salt and pepper, dot with bits of fat, if desired, and place in hot oven. As soon as flour is browned, begin to baste with cup of hot water every ten minutes. Cook until breast meat is tender, about 1½ hours for 4 lbs. fowl. Longer for larger fowl.

STUFFING FOR ROAST FOWL

4 c bread crumbs	1 t poultry seasoning or onion
2 t salt	¼ c melted fat
¼ t pepper	2/3 c boiling water
1 egg slightly beaten (if desired)	

Mix in order given, combine thoroughly and use to stuff fowls. If a dry, crumbly dressing is desired, omit the boiling water.

VEGETABLES

POTATO EXPERIMENTS

1. Grate a piece of potato, wash the grated potato with cold water and test a little of the water with iodine.
2. Test the residue with iodine. Does it give the same result as 1?
3. Boil the water used in washing the grated potato.
4. Boil a potato in its skin.
5. Pare a potato and boil in boiling salted water.
6. Pare a potato and put it over to cook in cold water.
7. Compare the results gained in 5, 6, and 7 as to color, texture and time required in cooking.

BOILED POTATOES

Select potatoes according to method of preparation. If cooked in the "jackets" the potatoes should be uniform in size, and with smooth skins, free from blemish. If pared, and plain boiled, they should again be uniform in size and not too large, and the potatoes selected should be in good condition. If, however, they are to be mashed, riced, creamed or scalloped, potatoes of different sizes and those with the blemishes can be used, and cut into smaller sections for boiling.

Wash potatoes before paring. Use sharp, well-pointed knife, pare potatoes thin, and carefully remove all eyes or specks. Place in cold water until all are ready. Drop into sufficient BOILING water to cover. Cover the sauce pan. Add salt a few minutes before they are tender. This requires from 20 minutes to half an hour.

Test them with a fork, or better, a steel knitting needle kept for this purpose. Drain water off and let stand in kettle on back of stove for a few minutes, having the cover partly pushed back.

MASHED POTATOES

1 pt. hot boiled potatoes	2 tb butter
½ t salt	¼ c hot milk, or more
spk pepper	

Mash with wire masher or put through ricer the hot potatoes. Add seasoning, quantity of milk used will vary with quality of potatoes. Use just enough to moisten well, but potatoes should not seem watery. Place over fire again and beat till light and smooth.

BAKED POTATOES

Select smooth, well shaped potatoes of uniform size, and not too large. Wash and scrub well with a vegetable brush. Dry. Place in a shallow pan. An old one may be kept for this purpose. Place it in a moderate oven, turning occasionally so that they may bake evenly. It will require about 45 minutes for baking. Test by pressing between fingers. When they yield easily to pressure they are done.

GLAZED SWEET POTATOES

4 medium sized sweet   ¼ c brown sugar.
   potatoes   ¼ c butter

Boil potatoes until partly done, or about ten minutes. Slice lengthwise and place in buttered dripping pan. Sprinkle sugar over potatoes, and over that the butter in bits. Brown in moderate oven.

POTATO SOUFFLE

1 c riced potatoes   1 egg
1 tb fat   ½ t salt
¼ c milk   ⅛ t pepper
1 t chopped parsley

Add fat, milk, beaten egg yolk, salt, pepper and parsley to riced potatoes and mix well. Cut and fold in stiffly beaten white. Bake in well buttered dish, or individual molds in moderate oven, till egg is cooked. Serve immediately.

CREAMED POTATOES

Prepare equal amounts of cooked diced potatoes and white sauce No. II*, combine, season and serve.

SCALLOPED POTATOES

Prepare half as much white sauce No. II* as potatoes to be used. Butter baking dish, a shallow one is best. Pour the white sauce over the sliced or diced boiled potatoes. Over the top sprinkle buttered and sifted bread or cracker crumbs.. Brown in oven.

POTATO CROQUETTES

2 c mashed potatoes   1 egg or 2 yolks
⅛ t white pepper   2 tb fat
½ t salt   ¼ t celery salt

Beat the eggs, mix with potatoes and add other ingredients. A little milk is sometimes needed if potatoes are dry. Heat mixture in a sauce pan, stirring; when it leaves the side of the pan, turn it on to flat dish; when cool, divide, shape, crumb and fry.**
Other vegetables may be used in the same way.

FRENCH FRIED POTATOES

Wash and pare small potatoes. Cut into eighths, lengthwise. Soak 1 hour or more in cold water. Take from water, dry between towels. Fry at 385° F. to 400° F. (10° less for lard) in deep fat till golden brown.** Drain on absorbent paper. Sprinkle with salt.

SARATOGA CHIPS

Wash and pare potatoes. Slice thin with vegetable cutter into a bowl of cold water, then finish as with French fried potatoes.

STEWED TOMATOES

Wash, then cover with boiling water for a few moments. This will loosen the skin and it will peel off easily.
Boil until well cooked up, without adding water. Butter, salt and pepper should be added. A little sugar and onion juice may be added if desired. May be served on toast.

---

* See page 94 for directions.   ** See page 114 for directions.

SCALLOPED TOMATOES

1 qt. fresh tomatoes or 1	1 tb sugar
can may be used	½ tb salt
2 c stale bread or cracker	¼ t pepper
crumbs	onion juice or minced onion, if
2 or 3 tb butter	desired

Butter a baking dish, put a layer of tomatoes on the bottom, sprinkle over a little salt, pepper, sugar and onion, then add a layer of crumbs mixed with melted butter. Continue alternating layers finishing with crumbs on top. A shallow dish with fewer layers is usually better than the deeper baking dish. Bake until hot and brown.

BROILED TOMATOES

Firm tomatoes, not too ripe should be used. Cut in thick slices without peeling. Sprinkle with salt and pepper, dredge with flour or sprinkle with finely sifted bread crumbs. Broil or saute until brown in hot fat.

BAKED TOMATOES

4 to 6 tomatoes	1 tb butter
½ c soft bread crumbs or	1 t sugar
boiled rice	1 t salt and ¼ t pepper
1 t chopped parsley	

Select large, firm regular tomatoes of about same size. Wash but do not peel. Cut thin slice from stem end of each. Remove from center the seeds and pulp, being careful not to break the outer skin. Drain liquid from pulp. Mix with crumbs or rice, add melted butter and seasoning. Chopped ham or other left-over meat may be added. One-fourth teaspoon of thyme may be substituted for the parsley. Fill the tomatoes with the mixture, place them in a shallow dish and bake till tender, about fifteen minutes. If over-done, they fall to pieces.

BEETS

Wash and scrub thoroughly, but do not cut them as that destroys the flavor and color. Cook in boiling water until tender. Young beets require about an hour. Fall beets often take four or five hours. When cooked, place them in cold water and rub off the skin. They may then be sliced or cubed, and served hot with butter (about 1 tb to the cup of vegetable), salt and pepper; or they may be pickled in plain or spiced vinegar and served cold. Like other vegetables they may also be served in white or brown sauce; or sauted in a little butter or drippings; or combined with others and served as a salad.

The tender leaves of new beets may bo used as greens. To prepare, they should be washed carefully, placed in a small amount of boiling water, cooked till tender, drained well. Butter, salt and pepper are then added.

CARROTS

These should be washed, then scraped. If young, they may be cooked whole. The larger, older ones may be cut in slices, strips or cubes, placed in boiling water and cooked until tender. Only sufficient water to cover and cook the carrots should be used. Water may be drained off or used in preparation of white sauce, if desired.

Carrots may also be served with butter, 1 tb to 1 c vegetable, salt and pepper added. Chopped parsley may be used with them. For variety, season with sugar and lemon juice. They may also be sauteed or used as a salad.

Carrots are often boiled with meat, corned beef, fresh beef or mutton. The young ones may be baked in the pan with roast of beef or mutton, if desired.

ONIONS—STUFFED

10 medium onions	½ c white sauce
½ c chopped ham or nuts	½ c bread crumbs
½ c chopped onion	salt, pepper

Remove skins from onions and parboil ten minutes in uncovered kettle in boiling, salted water. Turn upside down to cool. Remove part of centers, or centers may be cut out before onions are boiled. Fill with chopped meat, onion, white sauce,* bread crumbs, and seasonings which have been well mixed. Place in a shallow, buttered baking pan, sprinkle with buttered crumbs and bake in a moderate oven until onions are tender.

Any other cold, cooked meat, finely chopped, may be substituted for the ham.

CELERY

Wash carefully, using brush to clean. Scrape if necessary. Cut into squares or one inch pieces. Boil until tender, about 20 minutes. Add salt just before removing from fire. Serve with butter, or white sauce.*

TURNIPS

Wash and pare these, cut in cubes or slices (not too thin). Be sure that all woody portions are removed. Place in boiling water and cook till tender. Drain, or part of the water may be used in the making of a white or brown sauce in which they may be served, if cut in cubes. If sliced, they may be sauted, or buttered and seasoning added, or they may be mashed before seasoning is added. Like the others, they may be used in a combination or macedoine salad.

Sometimes they may be placed in a buttered baking dish, white sauce* added, buttered crumbs sprinkled over the top and browned in the open. A little grated cheese, or chopped green pepper, or chopped parsley may be adde to give variety.

CABBAGE

Remove the outer imperfect leaves, cut in quarters and remove the woody inner portion or "heart." Freshen in water. May be cooked in quarters, or cut in smaller sections, or cut fine. Cook uncovered in boiling, salted water about thirty minutes. The addition of a little soda reduces the odor while cooking and aids in softening the cabbage. Over-cooking renders it dark and strong flavored. Drain thoroughly, may be seasoned with butter, salt and pepper. White* or brown sauce may be added. Cabbage is often boiled with meat, fresh beef, corn beef or ham. Sometimes a few slices of bacon or salt pork are placed in the water in which cabbage is boiled. In this case the addition of butter and salt are unnecessary as the above serve both purposes.

SCALLOPED CABBAGE

Mix cooked cabbage with half as much white sauce.* Season well. A little green pepper or chopped boiled ham may be added for flavor. Place in a buttered baking dish, cover with buttered crumbs.' Bake until hot and brown.

* See page 94 for directions.

CAULIFLOWER

Remove the leaves, cut away the woody end. Cauliflower may be cooked in whole head or broken into small sections. In either case it is well to soak for an hour or more in cold water to which a few tablespoons of vinegar have been added. Place in boiling salted water, sufficient to cover, cook without cover on kettle. Boil till tender. Over-cooking makes cauliflower dark and strong flavored. Serve with white sauce.*

DRIED LEGUMES—GENERAL DIRECTIONS

All dried legumes should be carefully picked over, washed and soaked over night in cold water. In the morning place in fresh water. Add ¼ t soda to each quart of legumes. Cook slowly until the outer skins begins to burst. Drain, add more boiling water and stew till tender.

Butter, salt and pepper should be added before serving, or they may be cooked with a piece of salt pork or bacon, which gives both fat and flavor, or, white sauce,* brown sauce or tomato sauce may be added, following the usual proportion for the use of white sauce with vegetables; or legumes cooked very soft may be put through strainer and the pulp used in making cream soup.**

SUCCOTASH

1 c dry lima beans or	1 can corn
2 c stewed	⅛ lb. salt pork

Prepare beans and cook with salt pork cut in cubes. Let water boil down till beans are rather dry. Add corn, cook up. Season.

Fresh lima beans and green corn cut from cob make more palatable succotash. Take equal measures of each and cook together with pork for about one hour.

KIDNEY BEANS—SPANISH STYLE

½ c onions	1 c tomatoes
1 c stewed kidney beans	1 green pepper

Slice onions and pepper. Boil all together until onions are tender and much water has evaporated from tomatoes. Season well. A little cayenne pepper may be added.

—From Home Science Cook Book.

* See page 94 for directions. ** See page 92 for directions.

Spring Vegetables

SALSIFY

Wash thoroughly, and trim off root and stem ends. Scrape off outer dark skin, cut up, and put into acidulated water to keep white. Salsify may also be cooked without scraping. Cook in boiling water, salt when done, serve with butter, or with white sauce. It may be used for scallop and also as a foundation for cream soup.*

SPINACH

Wash thoroughly in five or six waters, looking over carefully. Trim off stems from older plants, use younger plants whole. Scissors are useful in the preparation of spinach. It may be steamed or boiled. Will require fifteen to twenty minutes. Use very little boiling, salted water in cooking; the less the better. Water in which it is cooked may be used if desired. Drain off, and cut or chop spinach. Drain in colander, season with salt and butter, using ½ tb butter to 1 c of vegetable, and reheat. Garnish with hard cooked eggs. It may be served with a tart sauce, or it may be packed into molds, chilled, garnished, and served as a salad.

SWISS CHARD

This should be cooked like spinach. When tender, drain in a colander, squeeze out the water, chop finely, season with butter, pepper and salt, garnish with hard cooked eggs, and serve hot.

PARSNIPS

Wash, scrape, and cook in boiling water until tender, about thirty to forty-five minutes. May be buttered, creamed, mashed, sauted, or made into croquettes, substituting parsnips for potatoes in potato recipe.**

ASPARAGUS

Break off tough lower end. Wash stalks. If of equal length tie in bunch, and cook in small bunches in boiling salted water, twenty to forty minutes, until tender. Cook in deep sauce pan, standing tips upward. The steam will cook the tender tips, while the hard stalk will be cooked in the boiling water. Or, asparagus may be broken into inch pieces, the tough parts being cooked first and the tender tips added the last fifteen minutes. The water in which asparagus is cooked may be used for white sauce or soup.* Serve asparagus on toast, with drawn butter, white, or Hollandaise sauce.

GREEN CORN

Carefully remove husks and silk and cut away the stem end. Put on in boiling water, and cook until tender, ten to twenty minutes, or it may be steamed.

STRING BEANS

Cut off ends and remove strings. Cut in pieces ½ inch in length. Wash. Put in boiling water and cook until tender. May be boiled with salt pork, bacon, or beef, if desired. May be served with butter or with white sauce.

GREEN PEAS

Shell and wash. Boil in small quantity water until tender, 15 minutes or more, depending upon size or age. Serve with butter or white sauce. Part of the water in which they are cooked may be used in making the white sauce.*

* See page 92.   ** See page 80.

Creamed Vegetable Soups

GENERAL PROPORTIONS

½ to 1 c vegetable sauce   seasoning
1 qt. white sauce II

GENERAL DIRECTIONS

1. Cook vegetable, dice or strain and add to white sauce. Season.
2. Prepare white sauce according to general directions.
3. Water used in cooking vegetables may be used as part liquid in preparing white sauce.

CREAM OF POTATO SOUP

1 c mashed potato   1 pt. thin white sauce

Make white sauce 1*, mix with potato, season with salt, pepper and onion juice.

CREAM OF TOMATO SOUP

½ can or 1 qt. tomatoes   1 qt. milk
2 t sugar   1 slice onion
¼ t soda   ¼ c flour
1 t salt   ¼ c butter
pepper

Stew tomato, strain, add soda and seasoning. Scald milk in double boiler with one slice onion. Add flour well blended with butter, cook thoroughly. Remove onion from milk. Combine mixtures adding tomato to milk slowly, strain, serve at once in a hot dish.

---

* See page 94 for directions.

White Sauce Proportions

	I—Thin	II—Medium	IV—Very Thick	III—Thick
Flour	1 tb	2 tb	4 tb	3 tb
Fat	1 tb	1 tb	3 tb	2 tb
Liquid	1 c	1 c	1 c	1 c
Salt	¼ t	¼ t	1 t	¼ t

METHODS OF COMBINING AND USE

1. INVALID METHOD. Scald milk in a double boiler reserving a small portion to mix with flour to smooth paste. Add flour to scalded milk, stir and cook until sauce thickens, about ten minutes. Add butter and seasoning.
2. FRENCH METHOD. Flour and butter may be blended together and added to scalded milk, stirring until done.
3. AMERICAN METHOD. The quickest method, is to melt butter in sauce pan, then add flour, stirring till mixture becomes foamy, but not brown. Add milk, continue stirring to insure smoothness, cook till thickened. Season.
4. White sauce I is used in preparation of creamed soups. II is used for vegetables and gravies. III and IV is that usually used for croquettes, meat loaves and moulded meat or fish.

TOMATO SAUCE

2 tb fat   1 c strained tomato
1 tb chopped onion   ¼ t salt
1 tb flour   ⅛ t pepper
Brown onion in butter. Proceed as for white sauce.

SALADS

GENERAL DIRECTIONS

1. Lettuce should be thoroughly washed, carefully examined for insects, placed in cold water, then each leaf dried and all wrapped in damp cloth, the larger leaves at bottom, and placed in refrigerator till ready to use.
2. Lettuce may be shredded by tearing with fingers, or may be cut into strips with scissors.
3. A thick paring should be cut from cucumbers. They may be sliced or diced, then placed in cold water. Care must be taken that they do not become water soaked, soft and transparent.
4. Radishes may be sliced without removing pink skin. They may be curled by cutting with sharp pointed knife from top toward root end in pointed, petal-like form, then with point of knife, paring thinly to separate pink outer skin, but without breaking from base. Place in cold water.
5. Celery must be carefully looked over, first cutting away root end, then trimming tops. Wash thoroughly with brush, and cut out decomposed or rusty spots. It may be cut in pieces as desired. It is usually well to reserve the inner "hearts" for table use. To curl celery, cut stalks into pieces about two inches long. Beginning at round side, and at one end, cut down half an inch, making as many thin strips as possible. Turn the stalk, and cut these slices in opposite direction, as thin as possible. Cut opposite end in same way. Set pieces aside in very cold, acidulated water, and in short time many of the shreds will curl over.
6. All uncooked fruits and vegetables must be fresh, crisp and cold. They must also be carefully dried, if oil is to be used. Cooked vegetables should be firm, that they may be cut in neat pieces of uniform shape and size.
7. Meat, fish and most cooked vegetables used in salads should be well marinated and cold, before mixing with crisp plants, and dressing.
8. Fruits, vegetables, meats, fish, cheese, etc., may be used singly or in combination, care being taken that combinations are suitable in flavor and color.
9. In salads of many ingredients, nutritious food materials are mixed with those that are used chiefly for flavor.
10. Salad dressing to be used must be well made, and adapted to ingredients of salad.
11. Salad material should be well mixed together. This is best done by tossing together with two forks (small wooden forks, if possible).
12. Combine ingredients just before serving.
13. Serve on cold salad dish or plate.

FRENCH DRESSING

¼ t salt	3 tb olive oil
¼ t pepper	1 to 3 tb vinegar or lemon juice

Paprika or cayenne may be added, if desired. Also, a few drops of onion juice, or bowl may be rubbed with slices of onion, or clove of garlic. ¼ t mustard may be mixed with other dry ingredients.

Mix dry ingredients, add oil and stir till thoroughly mixed, then add vinegar a few drops at a time, and beat till emulsion is formed. Or, ingredients may all be placed in a bottle and shaken vigorously together to form emulsion.

Pour over prepared materials and toss together until dressing has all been absorbed.

BOILED DRESSING

2 t mustard	2 eggs, or 4 yolks
½ t salt	1 c vinegar (weak)
2 tb flour	4 tb butter, or oil
spk cayenne	1 c cream, or milk
½ c sugar	

1. Mix dry ingredients.
2. Add eggs, beat well.
3. Heat vinegar to boiling point and pour slowly over above mixture while stirring.
4. Cook over hot water, stirring constantly until thickened.
5. Add oil, or butter.
6. Thin with milk, sweet or sour.

MAYONNAISE DRESSING

1 egg yolk	pepper, cayenne
½ t salt	1 tb lemon juice or vinegar
1 t pwd. sugar	1 tb vinegar
½ t mustard	¾ -1 c salad oil
⅛ t paprika	

Into a deep bowl put the egg, and add salt, sugar, mustard, pepper, paprika, cayenne, and one teaspoonful of the acid. Beat thoroughly with a good Dover egg beater, then add oil one tablespoonful at a time, beating thoroughly after each addition until one-half cupful is added and the dressing is thick. The oil can then be added in larger quantities at a time. Dilute with the remainder of the acid, adding this alternately with the rest of the oil. Beat vigorously all the time during the making. When finished, the dressing should be smooth and very thick. The acid may be vinegar, lemon juice, or both.

Whole egg may be used and the quantity of acid, seasoning, and oil doubled. The dressing will not be so deep in color.

ASPARAGUS AND PIMIENTO

Use cooked or canned asparagus in pieces about three inches in length. Garnish with diamond or other fancy shaped pieces of pimiento, or serve in ring of pimiento. Use any dressing desired.

TOMATO AND CUCUMBERS

Alternate slices of tomato and cucumber, or mound cubes of cucumber on slices of tomato. Cress and minced onion add desirable flavor.

STUFFED TOMATO

Select smooth firm tomatoes. Pare, remove stem end, and hollow out center. Chill. Fill with chopped nuts, celery, and cucumber, or any other combination desired.

BEANS AND CHEESE

Use canned or cooked wax or green beans. Cut into inch pieces. Celery, onion, green pepper or pimiento may be added. Sprinkle with grated cheese.

CAULIFLOWER AND BEET

Use the flowerets of cold, cooked cauliflower. Slice beet, then cut in cubes, diamond or other figures, using cutter, if available. Use beet as garnish over cauliflower, or beet may be chopped fine and combined with it. Use French or mayonnaise dressing.

MACEDOINE SALAD

Use cooked carrot, turnip, beet and potato. Arrange in small mounds on lettuce, each vegetable by itself. Use any dressing desired.

GRAPE FRUIT

Sections of grape fruit may be served with dressing in grape fruit shell, or on lettuce. Use French dressing. Pimiento, nut, celery, or onion may be combined with it.

SUGGESTIVE SALAD COMBINATIONS

In addition to the above, the following are suggestive. Many others may be used. Peas and celery; peas and cheese or nuts; spinach and egg; celery, cabbage and pimiento; orange, banana and pineapple; orange and celery; orange and nut; celery, apple, and nut; banana and nut; apple and cress; lettuce, onion and pimiento; egg and tomato; cheese and nut; gelatine with vegetables.

VEAL SALAD

Cut veal into cubes and marinate, that is, add French dressing and allow to stand an hour or more to develop flavor. Add an equal quantity of clean, crisp celery, cut into small cubes. Just before serving mix with dressing and place some on top. About one cup of mayonnaise to one quart of mixture will be required. Nuts or peas may be added, if desired. Garnish with hard cooked eggs, curled celery, capers, or pickles.

FISH SALAD

Break fish into small pieces, marinate with French dressing. It may be combined with diced celery, or with shredded lettuce. Mix with a little mayonnaise, serve on lettuce leaves with dressing on top and garnish with lemon and parsley. Sliced hard boiled egg, peas, nuts, or green peppers may be combined with fish. Boiled dressing may be used in place of mayonnaise.

POTATO SALAD

2 c freshly boiled potatoes	1 tb finely minced parsley
1 t salt	about 3 tb olive oil
⅛ t pepper	1 tb vinegar
few drops onion juice	

Cut potatoes in half inch cubes. Add seasoning, then olive oil, only what the potatoes will absorb, then add vinegar and mix carefully until it is absorbed. Mound on a bed of lettuce in a shallow dish. Egg yolks make an attractive garnish if put through a ricer.

POTATO SALAD II

Add boiled dressing to cold diced potatoes. Diced hard boiled eggs and sliced cucumbers may be added to potatoes. Serve on bed of lettuce and garnish with parsley and minced egg. Thick cream may be stirred in. Diced beets may be used as a garnish.

EGG SALAD

I. Cut the whites of hard cooked eggs into eighths lengthwise, arrange on lettuce to simulate the petals of a flower. Put yolks through ricer and arrange in the center of whites. Serve with boiled dressing.

II. Cut egg lengthwise in quarters and serve on lettuce with boiled dressing.

III. Chop whites finely and arrange on lettuce. Put yolk through ricer and mound in the center. Serve with boiled dressing.

STUFFED OR DEVILED EGGS

Cut hard cooked eggs crosswise or lengthwise, remove yolks, mix with vinegar and seasoning, or with boiled dressing. Refill yolks in the whites. Cold minced ham or chicken may be added to the yolks. French dressing may be used instead of the vinegar.

CHEESE SALAD

Combine mild cream cheese with pimiento, shape into small balls and serve on head lettuce with French dressing.

COTTAGE CHEESE SALAD

Shape cottage cheese into balls and serve on lettuce, with boiled dressing.

SANDWICHES

GENERAL DIRECTIONS

1. Bread should be at least twenty-four hours old.
2. Bread should be cut thin and even. If cut in fancy shapes, crusts should be saved for other purposes.
3. In cutting bread, arrange slices so that they will fit together.
4. Cream butter until soft enough to spread easily. Spread bread evenly before cutting from loaf, unless fancy shapes are to be used, in which case too much butter would thus be wasted.
5. Sandwiches are best when prepared just before serving, but they may be kept fresh for several hours by wrapping them in damp cloth wrung as dry as possible; then surrounded with dry cloth. Or, they may be closely wrapped in paraffin paper. Lettuce sandwiches or those with moist filling should not be so preserved.

LETTUCE SANDWICHES

Dry lettuce leaves, spread with mayonnaise or boiled dressing, sprinkle with riced egg and place between slices of buttered bread. Lettuce sandwiches make a good substitute for a salad at a home luncheon.

CHEESE SANDWICHES

I. Put cream cheese through a ricer or chop fine. Use for filling.

II. Put soft, rich cheese through a ricer or chop fine; for each cupful use one egg yolk and two tablespoons of milk. Mix thoroughly and season to suit taste. Spread between thin slices of bread, pressing them well together, then cut into strips. Beat white of egg with one cup of milk, dip the sandwiches in this, drain them and saute in butter. —From Home Science Cook Book.

BREAD AND BUTTER FOLDS

Spread bread with butter, cut in thin slices, remove crusts and put slices together in pairs, cut in squares or triangles. May use white, entire wheat or brown bread. Three layer sandwiches may be made by placing a slice of brown bread between two slices of white bread.

MEAT SANDWICHES

Any cooked meat may be used. Ham, chicken, and beef are most desirable. Chop meat, or cut into very thin slices. Slices of olives, or pickles, and salad dressing may be added. Place between slices of bread. Do not spread filling too close to edges of bread.

Other sandwich fillings are: onions and cheese; ground peanuts; pimiento and nuts; nut and cheese; anchovy and cheese; sardine; egg; caviar; oyster; lobster; ham and egg; parsley and pimiento; and various kinds of sweet sandwiches, such as jams, jellies, marmalades, or ground dates or figs.

CAKES AND COOKIES

TEMPERATURE FOR BAKING CAKES

Angel Food ....355° F. for 40 min.
Sponge Cake ....355° F. for 40 min.
Loaf Cakes ....360° F. for 45 min.
Layer Cakes ....380° F. for 30 to 35 min.
Cup Cakes ....415° F. for 25 to 30 min.
Chocolate and Molasses Mixtures....350° to 400° F. for 30 to 45 min.

TEMPERATURES FOR BAKING COOKIES

Rolled Cookies...430° F. for 15 min.
Dropped Cookies ....400° F. for 20 to 25 min.

SCORE CARD FOR LOAF CAKES

GENERAL APPEARANCE—
  Size 5
  Shape 10
  Color 5
  Surface 5
FLAVOR—
  Taste 25
  Odor 25
TEXTURE AND INTERIOR APPEARANCE—
  Lightness 5
  Tenderness 5
  Elasticity 5
  Grain 5
  Color 5

  Total 100

SCORE CARD FOR LAYER CAKES

GENERAL APPEARANCE—
  Size 5
  Shape 5
  Surface 5
LAYERS—
  Thickness 10
  Flavor 15
  Texture 10
FILLING—
  Consistency 10
  Suitability 5
  Flavor 5
  Thickness 5
  Color 2
  Surface 3
COMBINED FLAVOR 20

  Total 100
—Taken from Matteson and Newlands "Laboratory
Manual of Foods and Cookery."

PLAIN CAKE

¼ c shortening	2 t baking powder
¾ c sugar	½ c milk
2 eggs	½ t flavoring
1½ c flour	

Rub shortening to cream. Mix in sugar gradually. Separate whites and yolks of eggs. Beat yolks till light, add to creamed butter and sugar. Sift together remaining dry ingredients. Add these alternately with milk, beating thoroughly. Flavor with vanilla. Beat egg whites till stiff and fold these into batter.

Have cake pan previously greased and lightly floured. Fill two-thirds full with mixture, having it little lower in center than toward sides.

The oven should be moderately hot, increasing in heat slightly during first part of baking.

According to Mrs. Lincoln, the time for baking a cake may be divided into four parts. During first part, the cake rises, but does not brown. In second quarter, it continues to rise, browns in specks. Third, it rises toward center, browns all over. Fourth, settles and shrinks from pan.

GOLD CAKE

½ c shortening	1¾ c flour
1 c sugar	3 t baking powder
8 to 10 egg yolks	¼ t salt
½ c milk	1 t orange extract

Mix according to directions for butter cake previously given.

Any plain cake recipe may be varied to make a yellow or gold cake by substituting 2 or 3 yolks for each egg used, or better, use 3 yolks and one white for each two eggs. In the same way, white cake may be made by substituting two whites for each egg required. The flavoring may be vanilla or lemon, or combination of these, almond, or any other desired.

May be baked in loaf, layers, or muffin pans.

SOUR CREAM CAKE

2 eggs	¼ t soda
1 c sugar	1 t baking powder
1 c sour cream	⅛ t ground nutmeg
1½ c flour	½ t lemon extract

Separate eggs. Beat yolks till light and lemon colored. Add sugar, beating well. Sift together dry ingredients, and stir in, alternately with milk. Add extract. Beat egg whites stiff and dry, and fold in. Bake in shallow pan, or muffin pans.

SPICE CAKE

¾ c shortening	1 t mixed allspice, nutmeg, cloves
1 c brown sugar	1 t cinnamon
3 eggs	spk ground mace
¾ c water	½ c raisins
¼ t soda	¼ c currants
3 c flour	¼ c citron

Mix as for other butter cakes. All dry ingredients should be sifted together. Raisins and currants should be chopped, or cut up fine. Citron will cut up more easily if first softened by steaming over hot water. Part of flour must be reserved to sift over fruit, which should be well beaten in, before stiff egg whites are folded in. Bake in loaf or tube pan, in very moderate oven, for about an hour. It is usually well to line pan with several thicknesses of greased paper.

Whites may be substituted for part of fruit. A cheaper shortening than butter can very well be used as shortening in all spice cakes. Clarified beef drippings or bacon fat give good flavor.

SPICE CAKE

¼ c shortening	2 t baking powder
¾ c sugar	½ t cinnamon
2 eggs	¼ t nutmeg
½ c milk	¼ t cloves and allspice
1¼ c flour	½ c chopped nuts or raisins

This is a plain cake recipe varied by addition of spice and nuts or fruit and the amount of flour used, slightly reduced to allow for this addition. Or 1½ c flour may be used and more milk added.

Mix as for plain cake, sifting spice with flour, a small portion of which has been reserved to sift over nuts or raisins, which may be added before egg whites are folded in.

SPONGE CAKE

4 to 6 egg yolks	½ lemon
1 c sugar	¼ t salt
1 c flour	4 to 6 egg whites

The general rule is equal measures of egg, sugar and flour. Number of eggs used depends on size. It will require six of medium size.

Grate rind of ½ lemon, and pour over the juice. Let stand, till ready to use. Beat yolks till thick and lemon colored, add sugar very gradually, and continue beating, using Dover egg beater. Strain lemon juice, add and beat again. Beat whites stiff, with wire beater. Fold part of stiff whites into yolks. Mix and sift together flour and salt several times. Sift part of flour over egg mixture, and carefully cut and fold it in. Then fold in remainder of whites and flour alternately. Be careful not to stir. Bake in slow oven, about an hour, if in loaf.

May be baked in tube pan, in muffin or lady finger pans, or in dripping pan for jelly roll.

A little powdered sugar may be sprinkled over top before baking, to produce flaky crust. 2 tb melted chocolate may be added to eggs and sugar.

COOKIES

¼ c shortening	½ t salt
½ c sugar	2 t baking powder
½ egg	¼ c milk
2 c flour	

Rub butter until creamy, gradually add sugar, then put in egg and beat together thoroughly. Next add alternately, the milk and 1 c flour in which salt and baking powder have been sifted. Add remainder of flour, or enough to make dough which will roll out well. If dough is well chilled before rolling it will be found to be more easily handled. Flour board slightly. Toss dough lightly on board to coat with flour, and prevent stickiness. Roll half of dough at a time. Occasionally, loosen dough from board with floured knife as rolling proceeds. Roll to thickness of ¼ inch or less.

Shape with cutter dipped in flour. Have a hot oven and bake quickly. Suggestions for variations in this recipe are given in Home Science Cook Book.

GINGERSNAPS

½ c molasses	¼ t soda
¼ c shortening	½ tb ginger
1⅝ c flour	¼ c sugar
½ t salt	

Heat molasses to boiling point and pour over shortening. Cool. Add dry ingredients mixed and sifted, chill thoroughly. Toss half the mixture on floured board. Roll thin as possible. Be careful to prevent sticking by loosening dough from board with floured knife. Shape with small round cutter, first dipped in flour. Place near together on a buttered sheet or pan and bake in a moderate oven. Gather up trimmings and roll with other portion of dough. During rolling, keep bowl with dough cool.

Be careful not to add much flour during rolling as too much makes cookies hard instead of crisp.

PEANUT COOKIES

½ c shortening	½ t salt
1 c sugar	2 c flour
2 eggs	2 t baking powder
¼ c milk	1 to 2 c chopped peanuts

Mix as for cake without separating whites and yolks of eggs. Add peanuts, finely chopped, last. Drop by teaspoon on greased pans, an inch or two apart. Place a half peanut on each and bake in quick oven.

Other nuts may be substituted for peanuts.

—From Home Science Cook Book.

VANILLA WAFERS

1/3 c shortening	2 t vanilla
1 c sugar	2 c flour or more
1 egg	2 t baking powder
¼ c milk	½ t salt

Cream shortening, add sugar, and egg, well beaten, then milk and vanilla. Sift dry ingredients together, and add. Use just flour enough to make stiff dough, that can be handled and rolled thin. Chill the dough. Follow directions for rolling and cutting previously given for cookies, except that these are to be rolled as thin as possible, the thinner the better. Use small cutter. Place close together in greased pan. Bake in hot oven.

SWEET MILK DOUGHNUTS

2 tb shortening	1 t salt
1 c sugar	½ t cinnamon or nutmeg
1 egg	flour to make a soft dough (3 to
1 c milk	4 c)
4 t baking powder	

Mix as a butter cake. Add 3 c flour mixed and sifted with dry ingredients, then enough more flour to make dough just stiff enough to roll. With knife, toss about one-third of dough on lightly floured board, knead slightly to make smooth. Roll to thickness of about ¼ inch. Use floured spatula freely to prevent dough from sticking to board. Cut with floured cutter. Fry at 375° F. (10° less for lard) in deep fat about 2 minutes. They should come quickly to the top. Brown on one side, turn and brown on other. Drain over fat and then on absorbent paper. When partly cool, or just before serving, sprinkle with powdered sugar, if desired.

SOUR MILK DOUGHNUTS

Substitute sour milk or buttermilk for the sweet milk, sifting ½ t soda instead of baking powder with dry ingredients. Use two eggs instead of one. Or, use ¼ t soda and 2 t baking powder.

If sour cream is used, omit shortening. Use ¼ t soda and the 2 t baking powder.

To make richer doughnuts, use 3 tb shortening and 3 eggs.

DEEP FAT FRYING—GENERAL DIRECTIONS

1. Use lard, Snow Drift, Crisco, or other vegetable fat, or part of these and part clarified drippings.

2. Use a deep kettle, an iron one is best.

3. Heat the fat till very hot, or until blue smoke arises.

4. Test by dropping in a bit of white bread crumb, which should become brown in half a minute for cooked food, or in one minute for uncooked food, like doughnuts or fritters.

5. Fat should be about 345° F. for batters, about 380° F. for croquettes and about 400° F. for Saratoga potatoes.

6. Use frying basket for croquettes, Saratoga potatoes, etc., but not for batters and doughs.

7. Have ready a tin plate on which to place frying basket while filling it, also a pan covered with absorbent paper on which to drain food when fried.

8. Place food in basket, or drop from wire spoon carefully into fat, being careful not to spatter.

9. Do not put too much into fat at one time as this lowers temperature.

10. Keep food under fat all the time. Avoid dipping up and down.

11. When brown, lift out, drain well over the fat and then on the paper.

12. To clarify fat after deep fat frying drop in a few pieces of raw potato and reheat fat, until potato becomes brown. Repeat if necessary, and then strain through cheese cloth, cool and cover.

CANDY AND CONFECTIONS

TEMPERATURE FOR COOKING CANDIES

Butter Scotch ....295° F.
Fondant ....240° F.
Fudge ....240° F.

PEANUT BRITTLE

1 c sugar   spk soda, if desired
¾ c peanuts

Put shelled peanuts, chopped if desired, on well buttered pan and set in hot place. Melt sugar, stirring constantly and with considerable pressure. When sugar becomes golden brown liquid, stir in hot nuts very quickly. Pour into pan and spread thin by tilting pan. If porous result is desired, add the speck of soda just before stirring in nuts.

BUTTER SCOTCH

1 c brown sugar   1 t vinegar
½ c water   4 tb butter

Boil together sugar, water and vinegar for ten minutes, then add butter and boil till "hard crack," (310° F.) that is, until brittle. Turn into greased pan.

FONDANT

1 c sugar   ⅛ t cream of tartar
¼ c water

Dissolve sugar in water, add cream of tartar. Have low fire. Boil slowly. Wipe crystals from sides of sauce pan with damp cloth on fork. Cover at first, as condensing steam on cover helps wash down crystals. DO NOT STIR OR JAR. Be sure there are no sugar crystals on testing skewer. Boil to "soft ball" stage, (238° F.) that is, a little dropped into cold water can be molded into soft ball between fingers, or until it "threads." Pour out on slightly buttered plate. Let stand, without jarring, until cool, then beat vigorously until it becomes white and creamy in texture. When cool and firm enough, knead until smooth. Wrap in paraffin paper and put in cool place until ready to mold.

MOLDING FONDANT

1. Factory made candies are suggestive of many shapes and varieties into which home made candies may be molded.
2. Divide fondant into as many parts as colors and flavors are desired.
3. Add color sparingly with toothpick.
4. Put in desired flavor in same way, at same time.
5. Knead in color and flavor.
6. Shape candies, making them small, uniform in size and attractive as possible.
7. Use fruit and nut (sparingly) to harmonize with color and flavor.
8. Colored fondant may be melted over water and used for dipping.
9. Chocolate for dipping should also be melted over water. Use candy dipper, or if not available, toothpicks or fork.

FUDGE

2 c sugar   2 oz. chocolate or 8 tb cocoa
½ c milk or water   2 tb butter
½ c corn syrup   1 tb vanilla

Mix sugar, syrup, liquid and chocolate together in a sauce pan. When sugar is dissolved, boil until it forms a soft ball when tested in cold water. Add butter and remove from fire, cool, beat until the mixture thickens, then add vanilla. Chopped nuts, raisins, or cocoanut may be mixed in before the mixture hardens. Pour into buttered tins, and cut in squares. Fudge may be kneaded as fondant, moulded and dipped in chocolate, or melted fondant.

FRUIT NUT PASTE

1 c dates   1 c shelled nuts
1 c figs   grated rind of 1 lemon
grated rind of 1 orange   very little orange juice, if needed
1 c seeded raisins

Pass the fruits and nuts together twice through the food chopper using the finest knife. Add the orange and lemon rind, also the orange juice if it is necessary to soften the mixture, but be very careful not to get it too moist. Press out about one inch thick on a board sprinkled with confectioner's sugar, cut into squares or diamonds and roll these in granulated sugar, and set aside to dry; or dip in melted chocolate.

STUFFED DATES AND RAISINS

Stoned dates and raisins may be stuffed with plain fondant or with nuts, or with little pieces of crystallized ginger, candied orange, or even sections of Brazil nuts, hazel nuts or almonds, whole or ground.

ICES AND ICE CREAMS

1. Freezing mixtures (a) 1 part ice to 1 part salt; (b) 3 parts ice to 1 part salt.
   Make each of these mixtures and determine the minimum temperature reached.
2. Prepare a recipe of lemon ice and of ice cream. Divide each into two parts. Freeze some of each recipe in both a and b mixtures.
   Compare results. Note time of freezing, consistency of product, fineness of grain and flavor.

GENERAL DIRECTIONS
Freezing
1. Scald can and dasher.
2. Pound ice in burlap sack, using wooden mallet, if possible. Ice should be pounded till well broken and nearly as fine as the salt.
3. Fit can, dasher and crank, to be sure that they are properly adjusted.
4. Use rock salt and mix salt and ice together in proportion of 1 part salt to 3 parts ice.
5. Pack well-mixed ice and salt about retainer, then fill retainer, not more than three-fourths full, with mixture to be frozen. Cover.
6. Turn crank slowly and steadily at first, then more rapidly as freezing progresses.
7. Do not pour off water while freezing mixture. Let drain off from bung hole and refill with ice and salt as needed.
8. When dasher turns hard, mixture is sufficiently frozen.

Packing
1. Wipe off cover very carefully.
2. Take out dasher.
3. Scrape frozen mixture down sides of freezer and pack down level.
4. Cork top of cover into which dasher fitted, and replace cover on retainer. It is usually well to place waxed paper over contents of can before replacing cover.
5. Draw off salt water.
6. Repack pail with ice and salt, using 1 part salt to 4 parts ice, well mixed.
7. Cover the whole closely with newspapers and let stand an hour or more to ripen.

ICES AND SHERBETS—GENERAL DIRECTIONS
1. Boil sugar and water to density of 28° about 10 minutes. Cool.
2. Strain fruit juice and add to syrup, bringing density to 20°.
3. 1 tb gelatine may be hydrated in 4 tb water and added, if desired.
4. Mixture may be partly frozen, then 1 to 2 stiffly beaten egg whites stirred in. Finish freezing.
5. Or, ½ c cream may be whipped, added to mixture when partly

frozen, then freezing continued.

6. Milk or cream may be substituted for water in which case it should be chilled before adding fruit juice.
7. Use juice of one lemon with each quart of fruit juice.

ORANGE ICE

1 qt. water	¼ c lemon juice
2 c sugar	¼ t salt
2 c orange juice	grated rind of 2 oranges

LEMON ICE

1 qt. water	¾ c lemon juice
2 c sugar	¼ t salt

STRAWBERRY ICE

1 qt. water	1 tb lemon juice
1½ c sugar	¼ t salt
2 c berry juice	

PINEAPPLE ICE

1 qt. water	1 to 2 c shredded pineapple
1 c sugar	¼ t salt
2 tb lemon juice	

ICE CREAM—WITH CUSTARD BASIS

1 pt. milk	¼ t salt
2 tb cornstarch	1 pt. cream
2 eggs	flavoring
1 c sugar	

Scald milk, reserving a little to mix with cornstarch. Add to scalded milk, cook in double boiler fifteen minutes. Beat eggs slightly, blend into mixture and cook few minutes longer, stirring constantly. Add sugar and salt. Cool and mix with cream. Add flavoring.

Different kinds of ice cream may be made from this foundation recipe. Mixture must be well chilled before adding fruit juices.

1 tb vanilla may be used, or 1 c maple syrup; in which case less sugar may be used.

1 to 2 c shredded pineapple, or the juice from pineapple, (use less sugar); 2 oz. melted chocolate; 1 qt. berries, crushed and strained; 1 qt. well mashed peaches or apricots; 1 c caramel syrup.

PHILADELPHIA ICE CREAM

1 qt. thin cream	¼ t salt
1 c sugar	flavoring

Scald cream, add sugar and salt. Cool and flavor before freezing. The flavor may be varied as in the ice cream with part custard, using the proportions given. If acid fruit is used chill thoroughly before adding.

QUICK FROSTING

1 tb milk or cream   ½ c powdered sugar

Add liquid slowly to powdered sugar, till consistency to spread. Flavor as desired. Spread on cake with wet knife.

ORANGE ICING

1 c powdered sugar   2 tb orange juice and the grated rind

Squeeze orange juice over grated rind and let stand for 1 hour or more. Strain. Add juice to 1 c powdered sugar, or enough to keep in shape when spread on cake.

Yolk of egg, or yellow coloring, may be used to deepen color.

BOILED FROSTING

1 c granulated sugar   ¼ t cream of tartar
1/3 c hot water   1 egg white

Dissolve sugar and cream of tartar in hot water and then boil without stirring until syrup taken up on fork or skewer will thread. Take from stove. Let cool slightly while beating one egg stiff. Then pour hot syrup over egg in fine stream, beating well. When it thickens and is perfectly smooth, pour over cake.

EIGHT MINUTE FROSTING

1 egg white   ⅞ c sugar
2 tb cold water   flavoring

Have water boiling in lower part of double boiler, put egg white, sugar and water into upper part and place over the stove to cook. Beat constantly for eight minutes, then remove from fire, add flavoring and spread on cake as it cools. Either granulated or powdered sugar may be used. A little melted chocolate may be added before removing from the fire, or, chopped nuts, raisins or cocoanut may be used.

PASTRY

PLAIN PASTRY

1 c flour	¼ c shortening
¼ t salt	¼ c cold water
⅛ t baking powder	

Sift together the dry ingredients. Baking powder may be omitted. Cut in the shortening as for baking powder biscuit. Use knife to cut or mix in water. The amount of water used will vary with the flour, so the proper consistency of dough must be learned rather than to place dependence on the measure of water. Dough must neither be sticky nor crumbly, and must be easily lifted from the bowl in one mass. If chilled before rolling, it may be more easily handled.

Toss on lightly floured board to coat with flour. Roll dough lightly, keeping in circular shape. Roll very thin. This will make one small double crust pie. For 9-inch pan about 1¼ c of flour required.

SINGLE CRUST PIE

Roll dough larger than the tin. Full rather than stretch over the tin as crust shrinks in baking. Flatten the crust to tin to press out air. If it is to be filled after baking, prick with fork. If for single crust pie, build up ridge to make greater depth and groove or "flute" the ridge in order that heat may stiffen it more quickly. If desired, crust may be fitted over outer surface of tin.

CUSTARD PIE

2 eggs or more	1½ c milk
3 tb sugar	nutmeg
⅛ t salt	

Beat egg slightly. Add sugar, salt and scalded milk. Line pan and build up rim. Strain in mixture, sprinkle with nutmeg. Have hot oven at first to stiffen crust quickly, then decrease heat and finish baking slowly.

RAISIN PIE

1½ c raisins	¼ t salt
2 eggs	¼ c sugar
1 lemon	

Stew raisins till soft enough to strain through colander. There should be about 1¼ c pulp. Add yolks, slightly beaten, salt, juice and grated rind of 1 lemon and sugar. The sugar may be omitted if desired. Cook up. Fill baked crust. Beat whites stiff and spread on top. Place in oven to cook and to brown slightly.

RHUBARB PIE I

1 pt. rhubarb	2 tb flour
1 c sugar	¼ t salt

Wash rhubarb, cut into ½ inch pieces. Mix with other ingredients. Line deep pie pan with paste. Fill with mixture, being careful not to heap up. Measure pan before mixing ingredients, so that no more may be prepared than pan will hold. May be covered with an upper crust, or barred with narrow strips of paste, or baked in lower crust only, and meringue added. In this case 1 or 2 beaten egg yolks are usually mixed with cooked rhubarb.

RHUBARB PIE II

1 pt. cooked rhubarb	2 egg yolks
juice of half a lemon	

Bake crust on inverted pie plate. Pour rhubarb, mixed with lemon juice and beaten egg yolks, into crust, and place in oven till eggs have cooked and thickened mixture.

CREAM PIE

2 c milk	2 tb cornstarch
½ c sugar	⅛ t salt
3 eggs	1 tb vanilla

Scald milk in double boiler, and slowly stir in cornstarch, moistened with cold water. Stir constantly until thick. Add eggs beaten slightly with the sugar, and cook a little longer. Add vanilla and pour into a crust which has been baked over an inverted pie tin.

The yolks alone may be used for the filling, whites saved for meringue. Put in slow oven to brown. ¼ c shredded or grated cocoanut may be mixed with filling before placing in crust, or may be sprinkled over meringue. 1 oz. chocolate, or 2 tb cocoa may be used for chocolate pie.

DOUBLE CRUST PIE

Fit lower crust as for single crust pie but do not build up edge. Have upper crust rolled out before filling is put in, or else lower crust will become soaked and soggy. The filling should not be piled high, but leveled to avoid cooking over while baking. Moisten the edge of the lower crust. The upper crust should be rolled a little larger than needed. Perforate, then place loosely, that is, not stretched, over the filling and press edges together. Sometimes for berry pies the lower crust is folded over the upper crust thus making a thick three layer edge to prevent the filling from boiling out.

DRIED APPLE PIE

¾ c dried apple	2 tb butter
¾ c sugar	1 slice lemon
4 to 6 cloves or ¼ t cinnamon	

Wash the apples and soak over night. Stew slowly without adding more water for several hours. Fill lower crust. Add sugar, lemon, spice, and butter placed in bits over top. Fit upper crust. Begin baking in hot oven decreasing the heat. If fresh apples are used, it will require from 4 to 6 for a pie.

DRIED APRICOT PIE

¾ c dried apricots	2 tb butter
1 c sugar	

Prepare as for dried apple
Other dried fruit may be used in similar way.

TURNOVERS

Use left-over dough.

Cut dough in pieces about four inches square. Place 1 tb lemon filling, jelly or fruit on half of dough. Perforate the other half with fork so as to allow steam to escape. Moisten edge with water. Fold dough into triangular shape, pressing down the edges. Bake. Other shapes may be used.

CHEESE STRAWS

Fold scraps of pastry dough together and roll thin. Sprinkle with grated cheese, salt and pepper. Cayenne may be added. Fold and roll again. Cut in strips 6 in. long and ¼ in. wide. Bake until crisp and brown. Cinnamon sticks may be made by substituting cinnamon and sugar for cheese, using four times as much cinnamon as sugar.

PUDDINGS AND DESSERTS

JUNKET

2 c milk	2 t liquid rennet, or ½ junket
2 tb sugar	tablet
½ t vanilla	2 t lukewarm water

Heat milk to lukewarm, (99° F.) in double boiler. Add sugar and flavoring, and stir until sugar is dissolved. Add rennet dissolved in water, and pour into dish from which custard is to be served. Let stand until cool and firm. Serve with cream, soft custard, fruit, or fruit syrup. Cinnamon, nutmeg, cocoanut, chocolate, cocoa, or other flavor may be substituted for vanilla.

SOFT CUSTARD

1 qt. scalded milk	¼ t salt
½ c sugar	4 to 6 eggs
	flavoring

Scald the milk in a double boiler. Beat the eggs slightly; add sugar and salt. Then add hot milk slowly. Stir mixture constantly until it thickens sufficiently to coat the spoon and the foam disappears from the top. Strain, cover, cool. Add the flavoring when the custard is partly cool.

The whole egg may be used, or yolks alone used, and whites saved for meringue. Prepare meringue by beating egg whites stiff and adding ½ tb sifted, powdered sugar for each egg. Drop by spoonful in shallow pan of hot, salted water, till egg white is cooked and light. Remove with skimmer, and place over soft custard, in dish from which it is to be served. This is known as "Floating Island." Meringue may also be used with firm custard, but instead of cooking over water, spread lightly over custard, and brown slightly in slow oven. Or, egg white may be folded into soft custard, which is made with yolks only.

For flavor, considerable variety is offered. It may be 1 t vanilla, or lemon extract, or ¼ t extract of bitter almond. Add these when custard is partly cooled. Or, omit sugar and substitute caramel. Or, maple sugar or syrup may take the place of granulated sugar.

Add 3 to 4 tb ground coffee to milk while scalding, for coffee flavor. Strain carefully. ¼ c cocoa may be mixed with sugar, or 2 oz. chocolate melted in milk, for chocolate custard. ¼ c cocoanut may be stirred in soft custard, when partly cooled, or into mixture for firm custard before baking, or cocoanut may be beaten into meringue, or sprinkled over it.

Custard may be served over fruit, and fruit juice, thickened and sweetened, used as a sauce. Peaches, berries, pineapple, orange, and bananas may be so used, as well as many kinds of conserves and canned fruits. The meringue may be flavored or colored as desired.

FIRM CUSTARD

For this, the ingredients are the same and in the same proportion. Scald the milk, add the beaten eggs with which the sugar has been mixed. Add also salt and flavoring which would better be ground cinnamon or nutmeg, rather than the liquid extracts. Strain into cups, rinsed in cold water, or into one mold. The custard may be either steamed over water or in a pan of water, or set in a pan of water and placed in the oven to bake at 250° to 350° F. They are done when puffy on top and firm in center, or when a silver knife, inserted in the center, comes out clean.

CORNSTARCH MOLD

2 ¼ c milk   flavoring
¼ c cornstarch   spk salt
¼ c sugar

Scald the milk in double boiler reserving ¼ c. Mix cornstarch with cold milk, stir into hot milk. Stir constantly until well thickened and clear. Should cook twenty minutes. Add sugar, salt and flavoring. Turn into mold rinsed in cold water.

CORNSTARCH PUDDING

1 qt. scalded milk   ¼ t salt
¼ c cornstarch   2 to 3 eggs
½ c sugar or substitute   Flavoring

Prepare and cook as for cornstarch mold, previously given. When cornstarch is well cooked, blend in beaten eggs. Yolks only may be used, and stiffly beaten whites folded in when cornstarch mixture has cooled, or whites may be used as meringue. Or, more cornstarch may be used for thickening and eggs omitted; or, stiff whites may be folded in. This is often called "Blanc Mange." Instead of all milk, half fruit syrup may be used. A few drops of color extract may be added to secure pudding of desired color, or meringue may be colored.

Chocolate, vanilla, cocoanut, caramel, maple, etc., may be used as flavors.

BREAD PUDDING

1 qt. scalded milk   ½ c sugar
1 c dry or   ¼ t salt
2 c stale crumbs   2 to 4 eggs

Soak crumbs in milk, add sugar, salt, and beaten eggs, also 1 tb butter, if desired. Pour in buttered, shallow baking dish, bake in moderate oven till firm, using test for firm custard; or steam, if desired, using steamer, or placing in pan of water, kept hot but not boiling.

Many variations are possible. Any of those suggested for custards may be used, or, 1 c raisins, figs, dates, or nuts may be stirred in before baking. Candied ginger, orange, or lemon peel may be used in same way. Jelly or conserve may be spread over top before meringue is added. A tart jelly, like plum or currant, is especially palatable. 2 t mixed spices may be used, allspice, cinnamon, nutmeg, cloves, and ginger, if desired. Molasses may be substituted for part of sugar. Bread pudding should be creamy in texture, not solid.

RICE PUDDING I

1 qt. scalded milk   ¼ t salt
1 c boiled rice   2 to 4 eggs
½ c sugar   (

Rice may be cooked in water or milk. Stir into milk, add sugar, salt, and eggs, slightly beaten. 1 tb butter may be added. Flavor as desired. Bake or steam in buttered shallow baking dish, till firm. Yolks only may be used. Meringue may be added, if desired. Many of the variations suggested for bread pudding may be used with rice pudding.

RICE PUDDING II

1 qt. milk	½ c sugar
½ c uncooked rice	¾ t salt

Stir well washed rice into milk, in buttered dish. Add sugar and salt. Flavor as desired. Bake very slowly, stirring occasionally, until rice is tender, and has absorbed all the milk. Will require several hours. Or, cook on top of stove for awhile, stirring often, then place in oven to finish cooking and brown.

TAPIOCA PUDDING

1 qt. scalded milk	¼ t salt
½ c tapioca	2 or more eggs
½ c sugar	

Stir soaked tapioca into hot milk. Continue stirring, and when it begins to thicken, add sugar, salt, slightly beaten eggs and 1 tb butter, if desired. Flavor with nutmeg, vanilla, fruit, nuts, or fruit juice. Pour into buttered baking dish, and bake in slow oven, until firm.

Eggs may be omitted, or yolks only may be used and whites reserved for meringue. Or, the tapioca may be cooked till transparent, on top of stove, in double boiler. The stiffly beaten whites may then be folded in before serving. May be served hot, or turned into molds, and served cold. Fruit sauce, whipped cream, or soft custard may be served with it.

APPLE TAPIOCA PUDDING

½ c tapioca	spk salt
1 pt. water	½ t cinnamon
½ c sugar	

Cook tapioca in boiling salted water in double boiler, stirring constantly until transparent. Then add sugar and spice, if desired. Butter a baking dish and place in it, cored and pared apples, whole or in sections. If left whole the centers may be filled with sugar, raisins, nuts or jelly. Pour cooked tapioca over apples. Bake until apples are tender. Serve with cream or soft custard.

LEMON JELLY

¼ box or 1 tb granulated gelatine	½ c lemon juice
	1 c sugar
¼ c cold water	spk salt
1 c boiling water	

Soak gelatine in cold water till well hydrated. Pour over it boiling water. Gelatine must be well dissolved. Add lemon juice, sugar, spk of salt (for additional flavor, a bit of lemon rind or 1 inch stick cinnamon may have been steeped in the water). Strain through cheese cloth over wire strainer. Pour in molds (not tin) that have been rinsed in cold water. Put in cool place to harden.

Less lemon juice and more water may be used, if desired. In this case less sugar will be needed.

ORANGE JELLY

1 tb granulated gelatine	juice of half a lemon
¼ c cold water	½ c sugar
¼ c boiling water	spk salt
1 ¼ c orange juice	

Prepare as for lemon jelly. The general rule for gelatine mixtures is ½ box or 2 tb gelatine to 1 qt. liquid. It will vary, however, with the different brands of gelatine and depends greatly upon time for thickening, temperature and fruit used. Too much results in leather-like jelly. 2 tb gelatine to 3½ c liquid is better for school recipes, where time is limited. For each tablespoonful of gelatine used, take ½ c cold water for hydration, and 1½ c of other liquid, part to be boiling water, or all fruit juice may be used, in which case gelatine must be dissolved over boiling water.

Six hours or more will be required to harden a large mold. It is usually well to prepare the day before serving. Small molds cool more quickly, and cracked ice and salt will be found an aid.

Fruit juices such as grape, strawberry, raspberry or fruit syrups may be used, and jellies of any flavor prepared. Or, wine, coffee, maple syrup, caramel may be substituted for fruit juice, or fruit or nuts may be stirred into mixture before it is turned into molds.

Gelatine salads are prepared in the same way, using celery, cabbage, or pepper, instead of fruits. Use about 1 c cut up fruit or other similar material for 1¾ c liquid. About 2 tb to ¼ c less liquid must be used for the solid substance added. Both salads and desserts may be colored. A little lemon juice brings out all other flavors. Use 1 lemon (or about 4 tb) to the quart of liquid.

ORANGE SPONGE

1 tb granulated gelatine	juice of half a lemon
¼ c boiling water	½ c sugar
¼ c cold water	spk salt
1¼ c orange juice	3 egg whites

Prepare as for lemon jelly. Turn into mold. Stir occasionally until mixture begins to thicken; then add, gradually, the whites of egg, beaten stiff and dry, and beat until the whole is very light, and stiff enough to hold its shape. Pile lightly in serving dish, and serve very cold with whipped cream. Or, sponge may be molded and served with whipped cream or soft custard. Boiling water may be omitted, and 1½ c fruit juice used, and gelatine dissolved in it over boiling water.

Strawberry, raspberry, pineapple, grape, or lemon juice may be substituted for orange juice and sponge prepared in the same manner.

In the same manner, any of the jellies, with gelatine basis may be converted into sponges. Or, whipped cream may be folded in, instead of the egg whites.

ORANGE BAVARIAN CREAM

1 tb granulated gelatine	½ c sugar
¼ c cold water	1 c thick cream
1 c orange juice	spk salt
juice of half a lemon	

Prepare as for jelly, placing over boiling water to dissolve gelatine. Set in cold place and stir until it begins to thicken. Whip cream, and beat cream evenly into gelatine mixture, part at a time. When chilled enough to hold its shape, turn into mold.

PINEAPPLE BAVARIAN CREAM

1 tb granulated gelatine	Juice of half a lemon
¼ c cold water	1 c cream
1 c grated pineapple	spk salt
¼ c sugar	

The only difference in preparation here is that pineapple, if not canned, should be boiled with sugar. Strain or not, as desired. Any of the variations suggested for jellies and sponges apply also to the creams, or half egg white and half whipped cream may be used, if desired.

VANILLA BAVARIAN CREAM

1 tb granulated gelatine	3 egg yolks
¼ c cold water	1 t vanilla
1 c milk	1 c thick cream
¼ c sugar	spk salt

Soak gelatine in cold water. Scald milk, add beaten egg yolks and sugar. Cook as for custard. Add gelatine, strain. Set in cold place and stir until mixture begins to thicken. Then fold in whipped cream as for fruit Bavarian creams.

Caramel, or maple syrup may be substituted for the milk and prepared in the same way. With maple, omit sugar. Or, cold strong coffee may be used instead of cold water, or ¼ c ground coffee steeped in the milk, then strained.

Two squares chocolate may be used instead of vanilla or any other liquid flavoring used. Any of the creams may be colored, as desired.

STEAMED PUDDING

2 c flour	½ c molasses
½ t salt	½ c sour milk
½ t soda	2 tb shortening, melted
¼ t mixed spice	½ c chopped nuts or raisins

Mix as for gingerbread or Boston brown bread. Spice may be cinnamon, nutmeg, cloves and ginger. It is unnecessary to use butter for shortening as spice and molasses cover its flavor. Fruit used may be raisins, currants, dates, figs, citron, etc. Any kind of nuts may be used or part fruit and nuts. Grease molds. This will fill six good sized molds. Steam 1 to 2 hours. Serve with sauce.

—Home Science Cook Book.

PLAIN PUDDING SAUCE

1 orange or lemon	1 pt. boiling water
1 c sugar	2 tb shortening
2 tb cornstarch	

Grate the rind of orange or lemon, or half of each, and squeeze juice over it. In sauce pan mix sugar and cornstarch. Pour in the boiling water and cook from five to ten minutes, till thick and nearly clear, stirring constantly. Add butter and orange, and strain.

The yolk of one or more eggs may be blended with sauce just before straining, and the stiff whites folded in after. Other fruit juices may take the place of part of the liquid.

—Home Science Cook Book.

FRUIT SAUCE

1/3 c butter or substitute	⅛ t mace, or lemon juice may be
¼ c light brown sugar	used
1 or 2 egg yolks	1 c fruit juice

Heat fruit juice, which may be juice of fresh fruit or syrup of canned fruit, in which case less sugar will be needed. Add butter and sugar. Beat yolk, blend into hot syrup.

SHORT CAKE

1 pt. flour	¼ c shortening
2 tb sugar (may omit)	2/3 c liquid, or less
3 t baking powder	1 egg, if desired
½ t salt	

Mix as for biscuit, mixing egg, if used, with liquid. It is usually well to reserve part of liquid, as amount of milk varies with kind of flour. Divide dough into two parts, shape each by rolling or patting out, to fit pan. Put in one, brush with melted butter, place the second on top; or bake in two pans if more crust is desired. Bake in hot oven, twenty minutes or more.

Separate layers, placing partly crushed and sweetened fruit (strawberries, raspberries, peaches, oranges, pineapple, etc.) between, and more on top, if desired. May be served with cream, plain or whipped, if preferred.

Sugar may be omitted from above recipe. Shortening may be butter, lard or other fat, or a combination of different fats. Liquid may be milk or water. Individual short cakes may be prepared by shaping with biscuit cutter. Mixture is sometimes made little thinner than for soft dough, beaten smooth, and baked in two pans. Or, if sweet cake mixture is liked for short cake, use Twin Mountain muffin recipe.

APPLE ROLY POLY

2 c flour	2 good sized apples
¼ t salt	¼ c sugar
4 t baking powder	1 t cinnamon
2 tb shortening or more	2/3 c liquid

This is baking powder biscuit mixture, only slightly richer. Less shortening may be used, if desired. Follow directions for mixing and rolling biscuits, but roll dough into oblong shape, about one-fourth inch in thickness. Wash, pare, core and slice apples. Place evenly over dough, keeping about one-half inch from edges. Mix sugar and cinnamon and sprinkle over apples. Roll up dough, as for a jelly-roll, pressing well together. Keep of uniform thickness. Place on greased pan, bake in a much slower oven than for biscuits. Will require about 30 or 40 minutes or more. Instead of making into one roll, dough may be divided into smaller portions and several smaller rolls prepared in same way. Serve with pudding sauce or sweetened cream. Other fruit may be substituted for apples.

APPLE DUMPLING

Use same mixture as for roly poly. This will be sufficient for six dumplings. Divide into portions, pat into circular pieces, one-half inch thick. Place on each an apple, pared and cored. Fold dough neatly about it. Bake or steam until apples are tender. Apples may be cut in sections, if desired, or other fruit may be used. Serve with sauce or cream.

FRITTER BATTER

1 c flour	¼ t salt
1 to 1½ t baking powder	1/3 to ½ c milk
2 tb sugar	1 egg

Mix and sift dry ingredients, add milk gradually and egg well beaten. Beat thoroughly. Or, mix yolks with milk, add mixed and sifted dry ingredients, and fold in stiffly beaten egg white. Two eggs may be used, and baking powder omitted. Less sugar may be used, or it may be omitted.

APPLE FRITTERS

Core, pare and slice two apples. Sprinkle with powdered sugar and lemon juice. Dip or stir slices into the batter. Drop by spoonfuls, and *fry at 390° F. (10° less for lard) in deep fat to delicate brown. Drain. Serve hot, sprinkled with powdered sugar or with fruit sauce, syrup or jelly.

Or, apples may be pared and cored, then cut in ⅛ inch slices across apple, leaving hole in center. These slices may be dipped in batter and fried.

BANANA FRITTERS

Cut bananas in quarters, prepare and fry as apple fritters, or slice bananas into batter and drop by spoonfuls into hot fat.

Other fruits, clams, oysters, or small sections of cooked meat may be covered with batter and fried.

* See page 114 for directions.

144

CANNING AND PRESERVING

FOOD PRESERVATION EXPERIMENTS

Putrefaction

Place in a series of test tubes a, b, c, d, e, f, g, h, with a little cold water the following:

a—small piece raw chopped meat

b—a little white of egg

c—¼ t bread flour

d—¼ t cornstarch

e—¼ t cane sugar

f—a few ground dried peas

g—¼ t melted butter

h—¼ t olive oil.

Cover each test tube with a cotton stop, keep in a warm place and watch to determine which will putrefy and in what order.

Effect of Moisture

Place a small amount of the following foods in dry test tubes a, b, c, d, e, f.

In a duplicate series place the same foods, but moisten each with water.

Allow all to remain in a warm place and compare at the end of three days.

a—dried crushed peas

b—oatmeal

c—bread

d—entire wheat flour

e—bread flour

f—graham cracker

Effect of Temperature

Place bits of meat in a little water in three test tubes. Put the first in the ice chest, the second in ordinary room temperature, and the third close to oven, stove or radiator where the temperature is high. Notice the rapidity of putrefaction in each case.

Effect of Boiling

Chop finely some raw beef and place in water, warming slightly, but not heating it to more than 130° F. Divide into two parts, place each in a test tube, setting one aside without further treatment, but bringing the other to a brisk boil for a moment and then setting beside the first. At the end of twenty-four hours, examine to determine if putrefaction has occurred.

—Taken from Matteson & Newlands "A Laboratory

146

Manual of Foods and Cookery."

GENERAL DIRECTIONS

I. Selection and preparation of utensils—
  (a) Agateware kettles are best; agateware or wooden spoons; stoneware or agate bowls; agate colanders and funnels. Use silver knives in preparation of fruit, when possible.
  (b) Select jars with fewest possible parts; those which are simple in construction, easily cleaned and filled; those which will not permit food to come in contact with metal. Examine carefully to see that jars are perfect.
  (c) Use new rubbers of good quality, soft and elastic, but not too thick.
  (d) Wash each jar carefully in warm soapy water, rinse, and place on a rack in boiler or large pan. Partly fill each jar with water, and invert in water. Heat slowly until water boils, and boil for ten or fifteen minutes. Do not remove a jar from the boiling water until the moment it is to be filled with food. Rubbers should be dipped in boiling water and adjusted before jars are filled.

II. Selection and preparation of fruits and vegetables—
  (a) Select clean, firm, not over-ripe fruit or vegetables.
  (b) Clean thoroughly, peel, pare or scrape as required, and remove bruised portions.
  (c) Cover with cold water until ready for use.

III. Methods of canning—
  (a) Stewing, best adapted for watery foods when concentration is desired; or for a rich, sweet fruit.
    1. Sterilize jars.
    2. Prepare fruit.
    3. Cook soft vegetables, e. g., tomatoes, 20 minutes. Cook fruits in syrup until tender. Steam tough fruits until tender; then cook in syrup.
    4. Proportion: To each quart of water use from one-fourth to one-third as much sugar, depending on acidity of fruit.
    5. Adjust rubber and fill the hot, sterile jars full to overflowing with boiling fruit or vegetable. Cover and seal, invert can, and let it stand until cool.
  (b) Intermittent, best adapted for vegetables and fruits not easily sterilized, when a natural flavor is desired.
    1. Prepare cans.
    2. Prepare fruit, and pack firmly to within one-half inch of top. Do not crush or otherwise injure soft fruits. Add sugar or salt as desired, and fill can full with clean cold water. Adjust covers, but do not seal. Place jars on a rack in boiler or kettle, add water to reach one-third height of jars, heat slowly to boiling, and boil 10 to 45 minutes, depending upon texture of fruit. When boiling, raise covers, fill jars with boiling water or syrup, adjust rubbers, seal, boil five minutes longer, and remove jars from kettle; cool slowly, and allow to

stand for 24 hours. Repeat cooking as on first day. Remove, cool, and let stand another 24 hours. On the third day, reheat as before.

(c) Oven.
1. Prepare jars.
2. Prepare fruits and pack in jars as in intermittent method.
3. Adjust covers, but do not seal.
4. Set jars of fruit on asbestos board in oven, and cook slowly for 30 minutes. Cook vegetables, except tomatoes, for 3 hours.
5. Remove from oven, fill jars with boiling syrup or water, adjust rubbers and covers quickly, and seal.

(d) Cold pack (from Farmers' Bulletin No. 839, "Home Canning by the One-Period Cold Pack Method.")

HOME CANNING BY THE ONE-PERIOD COLD PACK METHOD
Steps in Canning

After the materials have been cleaned and put into the shape in which they are to be canned, and containers have been cleaned and tested, the canning procedure for most products by the one-period cold pack method consist of five steps: (1) scalding or blanching, (2) cold-dipping, (3) packing, (4) processing, and (5) sealing. In canning berries and all soft fruits the blanching is dispensed with.

The products to be canned are blanched or scalded usually by being placed in a cheese cloth bag or dipping basket into boiling water and allowed to remain there from 1 to 15 minutes, depending upon the kind of product. In the case of greens and green vegetables, however, the scalding is accomplished most satisfactorily in steam, as volatile oils and other substances remain in the food under this treatment. Such products may be put into a colander, set over a vessel of boiling water and covered as tightly as possible. Better results may be obtained, however, by the use of a steam cooker.

As soon as the product is removed from the boiling water or steam it should be dipped into cold, clean water and immediately removed and drained for a few moments. The temperature of the water used for cold dipping should be as low as possible.

The product should be packed carefully into hot jars as soon as removed. In the case of fruits, boiling hot syrup or hot water is then added. In the case of vegetables, hot water usually is used and salt is added for seasoning. The scalded rubbers and tops of jars are put into place, the tops of cans sealed, and the containers are placed in a hot water bath, pressure cooker, or other similar device for processing.

Processing is the final application of heat to sterilize the product and is continued for a period determined by the character of the product and the kind of apparatus used. The containers should be placed in the processing vessel as soon as they are filled.

Immediately after the termination of the processing period, while the products are still hot, glass and similar containers must be sealed.

Jars should then be placed in a tray upside down to cool and closely examined for leaks. If leakage occurs, the covers should be tightened until they are completely closed.

Tin cans may be cooled by plunging them in cold water. When the packed containers are thus cooled, they should be stored in a cool, dry place not exposed to freezing temperature. Most products packed in glass jars will bleach or darken if exposed to light. It is well, therefore, to wrap jars in paper. From time to time, especially during very hot weather, both glass jars and tin cans should be examined to make certain that there are no leaks, swellings, or other signs of fermentation.

For processing, home canners may choose from among several types of apparatus, according to their needs and means.

HOME-MADE OUTFITS

Home-made outfits are constructed of such utensils as wash boilers, tin pails, milk cans, metal wash tubs, and lard pails. Such canners should have well-fitting covers and false bottoms on lifting platforms of metal or wood. The latter are to support jars or cans to prevent direct contact with heat and also to permit a free circulation of water and steam around and under the containers.

SEASONING

In seasoning foods it should be kept in mind that most vegetables as well as meats are injured in flavor and quality by an excessive use of salt for seasoning in the canning process. A little salt is very palatable, and its use should be encouraged, but it is better to add no salt in canning than to use too much. Salt can be added to suit the taste when canned goods are served.

SYRUPS

Syrups are employed usually in canning fruits. The formula sometimes called the Eastern formula is 3 quarts of water to 2 quarts of sugar, boiled to a thin, medium-thin, medium-thick, or thick syrup.

Thin syrup is sugar and water boiled sufficiently to dissolve all of the sugar, but is not sticky. Such syrup has a density of from 12 to 20 per cent.

Medium-thin syrup is that which has begun to thicken and becomes sticky when cooled on the finger tip or spoon (density of from 20 to 40 per cent).

Medium-thick syrup is that which has thickened enough to roll or pile up over the edge of the spoon when it is poured out (density of from 40 to 50 per cent).

Thick syrup is that which has become so thick that it is difficult to pour out of a spoon or container, but is not sugared (density of from 50 to 64 per cent).

Thin syrups are used for all sweet fruits such as cherries, peaches, apples, etc., that are not too delicate in texture and color. Medium-thin syrups are used in the canning of the medium-sweet fruits, such as blackberries, currants, dewberries, huckleberries, raspberries, etc. Medium-thick syrups are used in the canning of all sour fruits, such as gooseberries, apricots, sour apples, etc., and delicately colored fruits, such as strawberries, and red raspberries. Thick syrup is used in preserving and making all kinds of sun-cooked preserves.

VEGETABLES

TOMATOES. Scald 1½ minutes or until skins loosen. Cold dip. Remove stems and cores. Pack directly into cans or hot jars. Press down with tablespoon (add no water). Add level teaspoonful salt per quart. Put rubbers and caps of jars into position, not tight. Seal tin cans completely. Sterilize for the length of time given for the particular type of outfit used.

SWEET CORN. Remove husk and silk. Blanch 5 minutes on cob. Cold dip; cut corn from cob and pack directly in hot jars or cans (¼ inch of top). Fill with boiling water. Add level teaspoonful salt per quart. Put rubbers and caps of jars into position, not tight. Seal tin cans completely. Sterilize for the length of time given for the particular type of outfit used.

Corn seems to give home canners more trouble than do most products; but, with care and study, corn may be canned as easily as any other product grown in the garden. A little experience in selecting the ear and the ability to recognize corn that is just between the milk and the dough stage are important. Cut the corn from the cob with a sharp, thin-bladed knife, and pack it at once into sterilized jars. Best results can be obtained when one person cuts the corn from the cob and one person fills the containers. If it is necessary for one person to work alone, he should cut off sufficient corn to fill one jar, pour on boiling water, add salt, place the rubber and the cap in position, and put the jar into the canner of hot water at once. Corn expands a little in processing, and for this reason jars should not be filled quite full. Corn that has reached the dough stage before being packed will have a cheesy appearance after canning. Corn should never be allowed to remain in the cold dip water, and large quantities should not be dipped at one time unless sufficient help is available to handle the product quickly. Water-logged or soaked corn indicates inefficient packing.

When canning sweet corn on the cob, following same directions but pack whole ears in jars instead of the cut-off corn.

VEGETABLES SUCH AS WAX BEANS, STRINGLESS BEANS, OKRA, GREEN PEPPERS, CABBAGE AND BRUSSELS SPROUTS. String or hull. Blanch in live steam for 5 to 10 minutes. Remove and dip quickly in cold water. Pack in hot jars or tin cans and add boiling hot water until jars or tin cans are full. Add one level teaspoonful of salt to each quart. Put rubbers and caps of jars in position, not tight. Seal tin cans completely. Sterilize for the length of time given for the particular type of outfit used.

Remove from container; tighten cover; invert to cool, and test the joints. Wrap in paper to prevent breakage, and store.

PEAS. A cloudy or hazy appearance of the liquid when peas are keeping well indicates that the product was roughly handled in blanching and cold-dipping, or that split or broken peas were not removed before packing. When peas are too old and blanching is not done carefully, the skin becomes cracked and the liquid cloudy.

Some waters of high mineral content have a tendency to increase cloudiness, also to harden the peas.

ROOT AND TUBER VEGETABLES, such as Carrots, Parsnips, Salsify, Beets, Turnips, and Sweet Potatoes. Grade for size, color, and degree of ripeness. Wash thoroughly, use vegetable brush. Scald or blanch in hot water sufficiently to loosen the skin. Dip quickly into cold water. Scrape or pare to remove skin. Pack whole vegetables, slices, or cross-section pieces in hot glass jars or tin cans. Add boiling hot water until full. Add level teaspoonful salt to quart. Place rubbers and tops of jars in position; partially seal, but not tight. Cap and tip tin cans completely. Sterilize for the length of time given for the particular type of outfit used.

Remove jars from canner; tighten covers; invert to cool and test joints. Wrap in paper and store.

HOW TO PREVENT THE FADING OF BEETS. Small beets that run 40 to the quart are the most suitable size for first-class packs. The older the beet the more chance there is for loss of color. When preparing the beet, leave on 1 inch of the stem and all of the tail while blanching. Blanch not more than 5 minutes, and cold-dip. The skin should be scraped from the beet, not peeled. Beets should be packed whole, if possible. Well-canned beets will show a slight loss of color when removed from the canner, but will brighten up in a few days.

FRUITS

SOFT FRUITS AND BERRIES. These include, apricots, blackberries, blueberries, cherries, currants, dewberries, figs, gooseberries, grapes, huckleberries, peaches, plums, raspberries, and strawberries.

After hulling, seeding, stemming, or skinning the fruit, place fruit in a strainer and rinse by pouring cold water over it. Pack from strainer into hot jars or cans without crushing, using big spoon or ladle. Hot syrup previously prepared should be poured over the fruit at once. If using tin cans, seal completely. Enameled tin cans should be used for all highly acid berries. Sterilize for the length of time given for the particular type of outfit used.

HARD FRUITS—Apples, Pears, and Quinces. Remove skin and core. Cut into convenient slices or sections and drop into slightly salted cold water to keep from tarnishing. Blanch 1½ minutes. Cold-dip. Pack closely in hot jars or tin cans. Fill with hot syrup. Put rubbers and caps of jars into position, not tight. Seal tin cans completely. Sterilize for the length of time given for the particular type of outfit used.

SPECIAL CANNING PRECAUTIONS AND SUGGESTIONS
Mold on Canned Goods

Mold may develop on canned goods (1) if the seal is defective; (2) if after sterilizing the tops are removed from the jars to replace the rubber rings; (3) if the jars are kept in a damp place where the rubbers may decompose.

Shrinkage During Sterilization

Shrinkage may occur during sterilization because of (1) improper and insufficient blanching and cold-dipping; (2) careless packing; (3) poor grading; (4) sterilizing for too long a period; (5) lack of judgment in the amount and size of product put into the container.

Blanching Greens

The proper way to blanch all greens or pot herbs is in a steamer or in a vessel improvised to do all the blanching in steam above the water line. If this is done, a high percentage of mineral salts and volatile oil is retained in the product.

SPECIAL REQUIREMENTS OF CORN, PEAS, BEANS AND ASPARAGUS

Canned corn, peas, beans, and asparagus may show no signs of spoilage and still when opened have a sour taste and a disagreeable odor. This specific trouble is known to the canner, as "flat-sour," and can be avoided if the canner will use fresh product, that is, one which has not been gathered more than 5 to 6 hours, and will blanch, cold-dip and pack one jar of product at a time, and place each jar in the canner as it is packed. The first jar in will not be affected by the extra cooking. When the steam pressure cooker is used the jars or cans may be placed in the retort, the cover placed in position, but not clamped down until the retort is filled. Rapid cooling of these products prevents over-cooking, clarifies the liquid, and preserves the shape and texture.

CANNING FRUIT WITHOUT SUGAR

All fruits can be canned successfully for future use for jelly making, pie filling, salad purposes, etc., without the use of sugar by simply adding hot water instead of the hot syrups. It has been found practicable also with certain vegetables to substitute sugar for salt in the canning process, and then add other seasoning to taste when serving.

In canning fruit without sugar, can the product the day it is picked. Cull, stem, seed, and clean fruit by placing in strainer and pouring cold water over it. Pack the product carefully in hot glass jars or tin cans until full. Use tablespoon, wooden ladle, or table knife for packing purposes. Pour boiling hot water over the product in the hot jar. Place rubbers and caps in position, not tight. If using tin cans, seal completely. Place product in the sterilizer, vat, or canner, and sterilize for the length of time given in the table according to the particular type of outfit used.

After sterilizing remove the filled containers. Seal jars; invert to cool and test the joints. Wrap in paper to prevent bleaching and store in a dry, cool place. If tin cans are used it will be found advantageous to plunge them into cold water immediately after sterilization to cool them quickly.

CANNED PEACHES (Open Kettle Method)

Select firm peaches of uniform size. About 8 to 10 peaches are required to fill a quart jar. Wipe fruit, put in boiling water just long enough to loosen skins. Remove skins, cut in halves, and remove stones. Cook fruit at once, or cover with water to prevent discoloration. A few of the stones may be cooked with it for the almond flavor. Use one-quarter to one-third pound of sugar with about 1 pt. of water for each can of peaches.

Put sugar and water in preserving kettle and cook to syrup. Add fruit, cook slowly until it is soft enough to be easily pierced. Put fruit into sterilized jars, arranging outer surface of peach to the glass, fill to overflowing with boiling syrup, and seal.

CANNED TOMATOES

Wipe tomatoes, cover with boiling water, and let stand until skins may be easily removed. Place them in kettle and cook until thoroughly scalded. Skim frequently. Put in sterilized jars and seal. Salt may be added, if desired, in proportion of 1 teaspoon to the quart.

JELLIES
General Directions

1. Select clean, rather under-ripe fruit.
2. Wash fruit.
3. Cook in agate preserving kettle.
4. If fruit is very juicy, add just enough water to prevent burning, about one cup to four quarts of fruit. If it is less juicy, e. g., apple, quince, etc., discard any unsound portions, cut into small pieces without peeling or coring, and cover with water.
5. Heat slowly to boiling, crush thoroughly, and continue cooking until heated throughout.
6. Transfer to jelly bag wrung out of hot water, let drain into stone or agate bowl.
7. Test for pectin by adding 1 teaspoon alcohol to 1 teaspoon cooked fruit juice. If test shows heavy precipitate and juice is acid, the maximum amount of sugar may be used; with lighter precipitate, use less sugar.
8. Boil from 10 to 20 minutes according to amount of water added at first cooking. Skim well. Measure juice.
9. Heat some sugar in oven while juice is cooking. Stir occasionally to prevent burning. Measure the sugar, using from ¾ to 1 c for each cup of juice.
10. Add heated sugar to cooked fruit juice, stir until sugar is dissolved, boil from 3 to 10 minutes, or until jelly breaks off when dropped from spoon. The test with syrup gauge should register 25° B.
11. Pour jelly into heated, sterilized glasses, and set away to cool and harden.
12. Cover top of jelly with alcohol, or cover with boiling paraffin. Cover with tin or paper covers to protect from dust; label and store in cool, dry place.
13. A second and third extraction of juice may be made by mixing the fruit pulp with enough boiling water to cover, draining, and repeating process of jelly making.

CURRANT JELLY

Wash and pick over currants. Put in preserving kettle and mash with wooden potato masher. Follow general directions.

SPICED APPLE JELLY

1 qt. apples
1½ c cranberries
1½ c vinegar and water
Tie spices in cheese cloth

1 t cinnamon
1 t whole cloves

Cook all together, drain, and proceed as directed for jelly making.

QUINCE AND CRANBERRY JELLY

1 doz. quinces   3 qts. cranberries

Cook the fruits separately, drain, combine juices, and proceed as with any jelly.

CRABAPPLE JELLY

Wash fruit, wipe and remove stem and blossom ends. Cut in quarters, put in a preserving kettle and cover with cold water. Cook gently until apples are soft and clear. Follow general directions.

ORANGE MARMALADE

Select smooth, thin skinned fruit. Wash and remove any thickened ends. Remove the rind, including all of the white from the lemon. Cut up both oranges and lemons with a sharp knife. To each measure of fruit add three measures of cold water and set aside to soak in a granite sauce pan on the stove and boil 10 minutes. Set in a cool place until the following day, at which time measure the mixture and for every cupful, add one cupful of sugar, and one extra cupful. Put on the stove and cook until it jellies. One orange and one lemon will make 6 glasses.

GRAPE JUICE

3 qts. grapes   sugar
1 pt. water

Wash ripe grapes and free from stems. Measure, and to every three quarts grapes use 1 pt. water. Put into kettle and let come slowly to boiling point, stirring occasionally. Remove from fire and strain through thick cloth. Measure and put juice back in kettle. Add 1 cup granulated sugar to every 3 quarts of juice. Let come quickly to boiling point, and turn at once into sterilized bottles. If wild grapes are used, more sugar must be used.

SERVING

PREPARATION OF DINING ROOM

1. Inspect floor, and, if necessary, brush it carefully.
2. Air dining room thoroughly, and, if possible, arrange for good ventilation during the meal.
3. Dust woodwork, and furniture, using soft cloth.
4. Adjust window shades and curtains, so that the light will not fall directly in the eyes of any one at table.

THE TABLE

1. Note size of the table and adjust it so that each guest will not have less than twenty-five inches. Have table exactly in its place.
2. Lay silence cloth, which should be of white, thick, soft, double faced cotton material, made for the purpose. It should extend five inches over the end and sides of table, and may be fastened in at the corners, if so desired.
3. Lay table cloth straight and smooth, with central, lengthwise fold in exact middle of table. Table cloth should be of linen, immaculate, and with as few folds as possible.
4. Place centerpiece, if used, in exact center of table, and on it a low, simple floral or fruit decoration.

THE COVER

1. Have ready all silver required. It should be well polished, never dull nor finger-marked.
2. Have glasses glistening. Handle them at bottom.
3. Place knives at right of the plate space, half an inch from edge of table, straight, with cutting edge turned toward plate. Arrange in order in which they are to be used, the first used being farthest from the plate.
4. Place forks, with tines up, at left of plate space, half an inch from edge of table, and straight, in order of use beginning at outside.
5. Place spoons, bowls up, at right of knives, half an inch from edge of table, in order used, beginning at outside. Silver, for as many courses as desired, may be placed on table, and remaining pieces placed just before respective courses are served. Spoons or forks for serving, should be placed at right of the cover of the one who is to serve, or on the table beside the dish; never in the dish.
6. Napkins should be simply folded, placed at left of forks belonging to cover, half an inch from edge of table, with hemmed edge up, and parallel with edge of table and with forks.
7. Place tumblers just above knives, and slightly to the right. Fill three-fourths full just before meal is announced. Tumblers should be kept filled during meal. Do this either by pouring from carafe without touching tumbler, or by lifting from table and filling carefully, back of the guest.

8. Bread and butter plates, or butter dishes, are placed at upper left hand side of cover, at tip of forks. Lay butter spreader across butter plate, and supply butter just before announcing meal.
9. Individual salts and peppers may be placed in front of each cover; or salt and pepper shakers may be placed between each two covers; or near the corners of the table, on "plate line"; not in center of table.
10. Chairs should be placed up to table, but not under it.

THE SIDEBOARD

Sideboard should be covered with smooth, perfectly laundered runner. On it should be neatly arranged extra china, silver, finger bowls, etc. No hot dishes should ever be placed on sideboard.

THE SIDE TABLE OR "SERVICE" TABLE

Side table should be protected with a heavy cotton flannel cloth, and covered with linen cloth. On it may be placed a small tray for serving, and for removing from table small things and unused silver. Here should be placed hot plates and dishes brought from the pantry just before they are to be served.

SERVING

1. Have ready everything which is, or may be needed before announcing meal. Have everything in its proper place.
2. Warm all dishes on which hot food it to be served, by placing in warming oven half an hour before the meal is announced. Chill plates for cold food. Serve hot foods very hot, and cold foods very cold.
3. Announce meal quietly.
4. Have ready a small tray, covered with a doily, for serving and for removing from the table, small things and unused silver; another for removing anything not clean. Hold large dishes on a folded napkins, about six inches square, on palm of the left hand.
5. Serve everything from the left except beverages. In offering a dish of food be sure its spoon and fork are on the left toward the person to be served. Hold the dish conveniently near and low enough to be reached with ease by those at the table.

REMOVING A COURSE

1. Everything relating to one course only and not required by a later one should be removed. Take large dishes containing food first, then soiled silver, china and glass, then unused glass, china and silver, then other dishes belonging to that course only, then crumbs.
2. Remove plates from the left with the left hand. Remove glasses, cups and saucers from the right. Never reach across a cover.
3. In removing soup or salad plates, and even the dinner plates when there is nothing else at a cover, a waitress may take one in each hand. If a bread and butter plate has been used, it must be taken in one hand, the dinner plate in the other; if a juicy vegetable or compote has been served, she may take the dinner plate in her left hand and transfer to right hand, lift the compote dish with her left, and place it beside, not on, the knife and fork, then take the bread and butter plate,

thus leaving, as is most desirable, each cover clear as she passes around the table.

4. At a formal meal, never put one dish or plate on top of another. Small dishes may be set side by side on a tray.

5. After a course has been entirely removed, place silver for course which follows.

6. Fill water glasses, supply bread, butter, and other things as needed without being asked.

7. Remove crumbs between courses, when necessary.

Rules For Table Etiquette

THE INVITATION

1. An invitation to a meal should always be immediately accepted or declined.
2. If accepted, one should arrive at least five minutes before the stated hour, and greet host and hostess and other guests.
3. After a meal, the guest should remain for half an hour or more, and on leaving, should express his appreciation of the pleasant time to host and hostess.
4. When a meal is announced, one should go promptly to the table.

POSITION AT TABLE

1. Stand beside or back of chair until the hostess gives signal to be seated.
2. Be seated in chair from the left, and arise from same side. This prevents confusion.
3. Position while seated should be erect, with feet on floor, in front of chair. Chair should not be too close to table, nor too far back.
4. Elbows and hands should not rest on table. Elbows should be kept close to sides. Silver should not be fingered. One ought never reach across the table in front of one's neighbor.

USE OF NAPKINS

1. Napkins should be placed across the lap at beginning of meal. If a large dinner napkin, it should be kept partly folded.
2. At close of meal, napkin should be folded as inconspicuously as possible. It should not be lifted in the air, or shaken over table.
3. At close of a formal dinner, instead of folding, place the napkin loosely beside plate.

USE OF KNIFE AND FORK

1. The knife is used for cutting and should be handled with right hand, and held only by the handle. It should never be carried to the mouth with food.
2. Only that portion of food, which is to be eaten immediately, should be cut off at one time.
3. The fork is used for carrying all dry foods and many semi-solid foods (all salads, most desserts, most vegetables, omelets, soft cheese dishes, some fruit) to the mouth.
4. It should be held only by the handle, and should always be carried to the mouth with the right hand, prongs turned up. It should be held between thumb and first finger, with weight resting lightly on second finger.
5. It is also used for steadying solid food when cutting. The fork should then be held in the left hand, by the handle only, prongs turned down, palm of hand down, with first finger resting lightly on upper side of handle.
6. One kind of food only should be taken up on fork at a time.
7. Fork may be used to convey fish bones and other inedible portions of food back to plate.

8. Neither knife nor fork should be held upright, or used for a pointer, or in gesticulation.
9. When not in use, the knife or fork should be placed across plate at right side.
10. At end of meal, both knife and fork should be left in position on side of plate.

USE OF SPOON

1. Spoon is used for liquid foods only, and for those too soft to be conveniently handled with a fork.
2. It should be turned to the side when carried to the mouth, and food taken from the side. Spoon should never be turned to point into the mouth.
3. Dip spoon away from one, when serving with a spoon, or when taking soup.
4. Beverages should not be sipped from a spoon except for purpose of testing flavor and temperature, after which spoon should be placed in the saucer. It should never be left standing in cup.
5. Liquids should be taken noiselessly from spoon.

USE OF SALT SHAKER

1. When using salt shaker one should never pound it on table to loosen salt. If loosening is necessary, salt shaker may be rapped with hand.
2. When using salt from a salt cellar, salt should be taken out with a salt spoon, or the knife.
3. Celery, onions, etc., should not be dipped in a salt cellar which is to supply more than one member at the table; a little of the salt must be removed to plate for that purpose.

USE OF BUTTER

1. Butter should be spread with bread and butter knife, or case knife, and should never be taken with spoon or fork.
2. Butter should not be added to foods which have been already dressed, or seasoned.
3. Only a small portion of bread should be buttered at one time, never an entire slice.

USE OF BREAD

1. Bread should be placed on bread and butter plate, or on large plate, never on table cloth.
2. Bread should be broken, never cut, before buttering and carrying to the mouth.
3. A small piece of bread is often kept in left hand to serve as an aid in placing food on fork.

PARTAKING OF BEVERAGES

1. Never partake of beverages while food is in the mouth.
2. When drinking take a small amount at once time, and drink quietly.
3. Never cool hot beverages by stirring, dipping a portion out, turning the beverage into saucer, or blowing on a spoonful.

PROFFERING OR REFUSING FOOD

1. In offering to serve any one at the table, use one of these forms: "May I help you?" "May I offer you?" "Let me give you."

"Will you have?" is a form that should be used by waitress only.

2. In refusing food, do so by saying "Thank you, I do not care for any," but never say "I do not like that."

FURTHER SUGGESTIONS

1. Avoid making a noise in masticating or in drinking, and keep lips closed while chewing. One should eat slowly and masticate food thoroughly. He should not have finished the course while others at the table are still eating. Do not talk with food in the mouth. Never tip plate, soup plate, or any dish in order to remove last bit.
2. Bread should not be used to obtain last bit of gravy or sauce.
3. Never break bread or crackers into soup. In passing sugar bowls, glasses, etc., without handles, care should be taken not to allow the fingers to rest inside the dish.
4. If in doubt what to do, the custom is to glance at the hostess and adopt her method.
5. Never leave the table without being excused, unless when serving as waitress.
6. Toothpicks, like toothbrushes, should be used only in the privacy of one's room.

INDEX

www.ingramcontent.com/pod-product-compliance
Lightning Source LLC
Chambersburg PA
CBHW031439270326
41930CB00007B/786